"Susan Pease Gadoua is brilliant! Every now and then I come across a practitioner who really knows her stuff—first, because she has the credentials, but more importantly, because she's been there, done that! I highly recommend *Stronger Day by Day* to anyone trying to pick up the pieces after divorce. This book does an excellent job of normalizing the vast array of emotions that one feels during divorce, and the author writes in a way that lets you know she truly understands. It also calls on the reader to act esteemably, whereby everyone benefits."

—Francine D. Ward, speaker and author of *Esteemable Acts*

STRONGER DAY BY DAY

reflections for healing &
rebuilding after divorce

SUSAN PEASE GADOUA, LCSW

New Harbinger Publications, Inc.

Publisher's Note

*This publication is designed to provide accurate and authoritative information
in regard to the subject matter covered. It is sold with the understanding that
the publisher is not engaged in rendering psychological, financial, legal, or other
professional services. If expert assistance or counseling is needed, the services
of a competent professional should be sought.*

Distributed in Canada by Raincoast Books

Copyright © 2010 by Susan Pease Gadoua
New Harbinger Publications, Inc.
5674 Shattuck Avenue
Oakland, CA 94609
www.newharbinger.com

Cover design by Amy Shoup; Text design by Amy Shoup and Michele
Waters-Kermes; Acquired by Melissa Kirk; Edited by Kayla Sussell

---

Library of Congress Cataloging-in-Publication Data

Gadoua, Susan Pease.
  Stronger day by day : reflections for healing and rebuilding after divorce
/ Susan Pease Gadoua.
      p. cm.
  1. Divorce. 2. Divorce--Psychological aspects. I. Title.
  HQ814.G333 2010
  155.9'3--dc22
                              2010011985

FSC
Mixed Sources
Product group from well-managed
forests, controlled sources and
recycled wood or fiber

Cert no. SW-COC-000952
www.fsc.org
© 1996 Forest Stewardship Council

12   11   10

10   9   8   7   6   5   4   3   2   1

This book is printed with soy ink.   First printing

I want to acknowledge all those who have had the courage to get through the divorce process while also maintaining a sense of maturity and integrity. Divorce truly is one of the most challenging and far-reaching transitions anyone will have to make. This book is dedicated to you.

CONTENTS

ACKNOWLEDGMENTS

My greatest thanks go to my husband, Michael, for his love and support during the writing of this book and always.

I'd like to thank my friend and editor, Leslie Keenan, for once again being there in every way I needed her to be.

Thanks to Melissa Kirk and all the people at New Harbinger who entrusted me to write another divorce-related book. And to Kayla Sussell for her valuable feedback and edits.

INTRODUCTION

The first few years during and after any major loss are typically when the deepest grieving occurs. Divorce, perhaps the greatest loss a person will ever experience besides the death of a loved one, has its own unique set of grief triggers. This is primarily due to the fact that the person from whom you are parting does not go away completely.

In many cases, you will still interact with your spouse in significant ways, such as coparenting, dealing with extended family and house and home issues, and dealing with financial ties you may maintain. Moreover, as if that isn't enough, you may also have to deal with the painful feelings that arise when one of you finds a new partner.

This book is designed to provide you with frequent thoughts of hope, strength, and inspiration to move through the grieving process better, faster, and stronger than you might without this support.

It is written for the person who wants to get through the divorce process with integrity and self-esteem. Divorce does not have to tear people to shreds or wreak emotional havoc. Divorce with dignity is available to anyone willing to do the hard work needed to act from a higher, more mature place (which is within everyone) rather than from a lower, less mature place (also within everyone). To do this, you will need the skills—found in this book—that will help to normalize the process emotionally and mentally and create calm.

This book is a series of reflections. Each short chapter begins with a quote. Then follows the reflection itself—an elaboration or explanation of the quote intended to make it easier for you to apply the words to your own life. And, at the end of each section, there is an affirmation, written in the first person, to reinforce positive and empowering thoughts and beliefs. There is also an exercise—for example, a journaling exercise, a meditation, or both.

These exercises are designed to be completed following the reading, but you can omit them if you choose to, or you can skip the reading and just do the exercise or meditation.

The focus of each reading is purposely on you and you alone and doesn't address the needs of those around you. Some of the sections may apply to other people in your life, but it is important in your divorce recovery process to keep the focus of this major life transition on yourself.

This book is written for divorcing people at any stage of the process. It is for that reason that I purposely use the word "spouse." In places, I tried using "ex-spouse" or "soon-to-be-ex-spouse" but, along with being cumbersome, these usages assumed the reader to be further on than I thought appropriate. Feel free to substitute your spouse's name or whatever other word works for you. I chose to keep it simple.

You may want to read this book in the order it was written, flip through the pages randomly and land on any page, or consult the table of contents to look up a particular topic.

If there is a topic that has a specific meaning for you, I encourage you to repeat the affirmation throughout the day, meditate on it, and perhaps do some journal writing on it. There are places throughout the book that ask you to do some further reflection, but you can do this at any point, on any topic, anytime you'd like. If you have a therapist or you attend a divorce support group, you may even want to bring the topic up for further discussion with that person.

No matter where you are in your marital dissolution process—at the very beginning or three years postdivorce—I promise you, you will get through it; your divorce will become a distant memory and you will go on with the next chapter of your life. This book will help you get there.

1

INTO THE UNKNOWN

*One doesn't discover new lands without consenting to
lose sight of the shore for a very long time.*

~ Andre Gide

One of the reasons humans seek out the familiar is that it
gives us a sense of safety in our environment. When we feel
safe, we can focus on other matters; when we feel unsafe,
our primary focus will be on trying to regain that sense of
safety.

Going through a divorce strips most people of their sense
of security. The most obvious manifestation of this occurs
with finances. Going from being one of a married couple to
a single person usually means having half (or even less) of
the income you had while you were with your spouse but still
having the same amount of expenses (or even more). This
alone can be quite challenging.

There are other areas of your life in which your well-being
will also feel threatened as a result of having to let go of every-

thing that is familiar: the life you knew with your spouse, the routine you had with your family, your home, and your ties with extended family, and even mutual friends.

During your divorce, you may feel as though you are in a foreign land, groping in the dark, especially in all of these areas. To make matters worse, you have no knowledge of when the lights will be turned back on. The process often takes much longer than you think it will (or should) and you may have more questions than answers. You may not be able to see, even dimly, how things could possibly turn out well.

Losing your connection to all things familiar can be quite a jolt. We are creatures of habit and change comes hard for most of us. We also are not accustomed to feeling unsafe for prolonged periods.

It may help you to know that, in time, things will begin to make sense again and everything will fall into place. Even though your life may be quite different than it was when you were married, routines will return, a sense of comfort will come back to you, and most importantly, the sense of normalcy that you once enjoyed will be yours again.

AFFIRMATION

I will endure this time of unknowns knowing that my world will right itself in time.

JOURNAL EXERCISE

- *Describe the places in your life that no longer feel familiar or the areas in which you are experiencing many unknowns.*

- *How do you cope with these unknowns?*

- *What people or resources would help you feel more secure right now?*

MEDITATION

Take five minutes to sit quietly. Close your eyes and envision yourself where you want to be once your divorce is over. Think of how it will feel to be safe and secure again. Imagine how good it will feel to be settled into a new routine.

2

DIVORCE ISN'T EASY, BUT IT'S DOABLE

Divorce is the psychological equivalent of a triple coronary bypass.

~ Mary Kay Blakely

Getting a divorce is terrifying for the average person under average circumstances. Unlike other aspects of life, it does not necessarily get easier once you start the process. In fact, as you learn more about the legalities and finances, and as you get deeper into tasks such as dividing assets and debts, negotiating child custody, and addressing home, money, and job issues, it usually gets more difficult.

Just as you turn your life over to a surgeon when undergoing an operation, in a divorce you are asked to turn your well-being over to a number of different professionals, such as accountants, attorneys, and counselors. Having to trust these people with your financial and emotional welfare can certainly feel as though your life depends on their performance.

However, as daunting as it is, thousands of people divorce every day. The key to having a better divorce is to make sure you get all the support you need. For many people, this support is a divorce team that addresses their legal, financial, and emotional needs.

Although the process is not a linear one (meaning that it doesn't necessarily get better or easier with time), keep in mind that this ordeal will end, life will return to "normal" again, and you will regain your strength.

Just as we physically recover from surgery, our minds, hearts, and spirits recuperate from marital dissolution. It's a difficult process, even under the best of circumstances, but you will survive, and there is a new life awaiting you on the other side.

AFFIRMATION

I will survive this ordeal.

JOURNAL EXERCISE

- *On the left side of your journal page, write down the issues you face in your divorce (that is, having to sell your house, get a new job, pay child or spousal support). On the right-hand side, write down who the* members of your divorce team are (for example, the lawyer, accountant, mortgage broker, or real estate agent).

■   Now draw a line from the specific issue to the professional member of your divorce team. It is important to note that if you have any issues that lack a divorce team professional, this may be an area in which you are not receiving adequate support.

3

PHYSICAL WELL-BEING

He who has health has hope; and he who has hope has everything.

~Arabic proverb

When you feel well physically, you are much more capable of facing life's trials and tribulations. There are many things in life you cannot control, but you can decide how well you will take care of your health.

If you eat well, get adequate amounts of exercise, and get enough sleep, you will be more present to face the challenges that are inherent in divorce. If you don't take care of yourself, your problems will seem to be magnified.

Think about those times when you were sick or overtired and run-down from doing too much, but you had to show up at work, or for your kids, or at a social event. How present were you? How effective were you? How approachable were you? How enjoyable were you? And how much were you able to enjoy yourself? Our minds, emotions, and bodies are integrally connected. When compared to the times you feel well, your ability to do anything when you don't feel well is significantly diminished.

One of the ironies of divorce is that at a time when you may be emotionally and mentally at your lowest, you must make some of the biggest decisions of your life. This is all the more reason that you need to take care of your body and your overall health.

Getting even the smallest amount of exercise, such as a ten-minute walk, can help you to come back into balance with yourself. If you are storing pent-up emotion in your body, hitting a pillow for just five minutes can provide a much-needed physical release.

Exercise will make you feel better, stronger, and more capable; it can literally move the toxic energy out of your body. Eat as healthily as you can. Get six to eight hours of sleep when you can. Do everything in your power to make your physical well-being a priority as you move through your divorce process.

AFFIRMATION

I will take good care of my body today, and my body will take good care of me.

EXERCISE

Get physical! Here are some ideas: stand up and stretch; go for a walk; take a bike ride; jog; dance or sing; jump rope; swim; do yoga.

4

REACHING FOR THE SUN

It's not only children who grow. Parents do too. As much as we watch to see what our children do with their lives, they are watching us to see what we do with ours. I can't tell my children to reach for the sun. All I can do is reach for it myself.

~ Joyce Maynard

Whether you want to be one or not, you are an example to those around you: your friends, coworkers, and in particular, your children. On a daily basis, the things you say and do for others has an impact on them.

Most of us don't stop to ask this question: "What example am I setting for those around me about how to get through a divorce, handle heightened emotions, or treat people when I feel scared or angry?" But this is an important question to ask, especially if you have children looking to you to see how you handle the challenging matters you are facing.

It's not if you will have challenging moments in ending your marriage, it's *when*. What will you do about these moments when they come? If you are having a tough day, will you implode, explode, or take good, balanced care of yourself?

Some suggestions for good self-care include: taking a time-out when you feel that you need one, going for a walk, calling a friend, listening to soothing music, meditating, journaling, or talking to a mental health professional.

It's one thing to muddle through life's challenges when you have only yourself to think about. It's quite another thing to model how to get through pain. But knowing that how you act and react makes a difference to others may call on you to bring your higher self into play.

You don't have to be perfect. You just need to keep putting one foot in front of the other, doing the best you can, and asking for help when you need it.

AFFIRMATION

I will continue to reach for the sun knowing that others are watching me.

JOURNAL EXERCISE

- *Who are you setting an example for?*

- *Describe what you do to get through your divorce and handle your heightened emotions, and how you treat people when you are scared.*

- *Based on what you wrote above, what kind of example are you setting?*

- *Where can you improve?*

- *Who are the people and what are the resources you can call on to help you set a better example?*

5

RESTRAINT OF TONGUE
AND PEN

The morning is always wiser than the evening.

~ Russian proverb

Responding to a situation is always better than reacting to it. When we react to anything, it is usually with the first thought, word, or action that comes into our mind to retaliate with. If we are hurt, we often try to hurt back; if we are angry, we want to lash out in response; if we are left out, we want to reject those who left us out.

When things are said or done that hurt you, know that you do not have to respond immediately. You can sleep on most matters. When you wake up in the morning, you are likely to have a better perspective and be less emotional; you may even have thought through what you'd like to say or how to handle the situation in a way that will be more productive than your first response would have been.

Trying to hurt someone, especially your spouse, in retaliation for hurts he has caused you doesn't work. It may feel good in the moment, but that good feeling won't last long.

You are entitled to your feelings of anger, but lashing out at your spouse or kids is not the answer. More often than not, reacting badly just perpetuates a negative dynamic and the result is that everyone suffers. Divorce is hard enough without adding more layers of pain into the mix.

When you feel hurt or angry, give yourself time to calm down, call on your higher self, and respond (don't react). In those times when you feel a great deal of anger, find a safe, healthy outlet for discharging it, such as exercising, singing, crying, screaming into a pillow, journaling, or talking to someone about it.

AFFIRMATION

When I am upset, I will bite my tongue, walk away, and revisit the situation when I am calmer.

JOURNAL EXERCISE

■ *Write down three to five things that your spouse has said or done that have really hurt you.*

■ *Next, write out how you'd really like to react (you can be as graphic as you'd like here).*

■ *Finally, write out some different ways you can respond to the situation that will maintain your sense of integrity and be more productive.*

6

SHARING YOUR PAIN

There is no grief like the grief that does not speak.

~ Henry Wadsworth Longfellow

Although there is no one right way to deal with your grief while you are going through the dissolution of your marriage, some coping skills are better than others. Talking with someone about your feelings can help the grieving process to keep moving, and not talking to anyone—that is, not wanting to deal with what you're feeling—prevents you from moving on. This is so for a number of reasons.

In order for grief to pass, it must be acknowledged. Like a small child who tugs at your sleeve in an attempt to get your attention, your emotions need to be "heard." If you ignore the child, she doesn't stop tugging on you or trying to get your attention. She may, in fact, tug harder and may even start yelling! Emotions are much the same. They don't go away simply because you don't want to feel them or they are inconvenient.

Experiencing pain, sadness, and loneliness but not expressing them keeps you stuck, because you become emotionally clogged with whatever emotion you are not allowing yourself to feel. Talking about your pain is a way to acknowledge it.

Sharing your sadness with someone else can also bring you a new perspective on your situation. In some instances, hearing yourself tell your story can shine a light on your problem in a new way. For example, one woman described how hearing herself complain over and over again eventually helped her to realize that she didn't want to identify herself by her pain any longer. Hearing herself was the catalyst she needed to move to the next phase of her recovery, because she didn't want to become stuck in her painful story.

There's also something very powerful about being witnessed by another person as you grieve. Having someone simply listen to you can have a profound impact on helping you heal.

Moreover, it's important to seek out people who can and want to be there for you. If you don't feel safe and supported at this tumultuous time in your life, you will stop reaching out to others. If you are afraid of overburdening others, seek out more than one source of support. Perhaps you can find a divorce support group, a therapist, a new friend, or a relative. You cannot afford to lean on people who are not supportive, even if you think they "should" be.

Talking isn't the only way to heal, but it is an important tool to use in your divorce recovery.

AFFIRMATION

I share my grief with those who want to help and support me through this transition.

EXERCISE

Create the habit of calling or getting together with someone you feel comfortable talking to about your marriage's dissolution. You might start with sharing something less personal and see how that feels, and then work your way up to saying more. If you don't want to burden one friend, contact someone else.

If telling your friends feels too awkward or too much of an imposition, seek out a therapist who specializes in divorce and who understands the grief process.

Resources that cost little or no money include the clergy and self-help support groups such as twelve-step recovery groups.

7

STAGES OF GRIEF

*Only those who avoid love can avoid grief. The point is to
learn from grief and remain vulnerable to love.*

~ John Brantner

With any loss of a marriage comes grief. This is true regardless of the specific circumstances of your situation. Elisabeth
Kübler-Ross, a pioneer in understanding the area of grief,
laid out the five emotional and mental stages that follow a
great loss as being denial, anger, bargaining, depression, and,
finally, acceptance in that order.

During the grief process, you may not feel fully yourself
because you are likely to be preoccupied with one or more of
these intense stages of grieving, while also trying to keep up
with the events of your current life and figure out what lies
ahead.

Grief is inconvenient to say the least. Most of us would
rather just skip this part of divorce and move right into the
rebuilding. However, you cannot do this. You must go through

each and every stage of your grief process before you can truly move on.

The process does not necessarily move in a straight line, nor are you automatically done with a stage once you've experienced it. It's possible to go around and around all five stages, and you may even experience two or more stages at the same time.

For example, you may accept the loss of your relationship with your spouse but be unable to accept the loss of your dream of living "happily ever after," or you may be angry at a particular situation and think constantly about how and why it should be different (bargaining).

How long your grieving process will take depends on a variety of factors. To some degree, it will depend on how you manage your grief—do you allow yourself to feel all of your feelings or do you try to make your painful emotions go away?

How long it lasts also depends on the length of your marriage, the quality of your marriage, whether you were the leaver or the one left, whether you saw this coming, whether another person is involved, whether you have children, and how much support and other resources you have access to. This list could go on and on.

The more you learn about grief and about yourself, the better you will do. Divorce is almost never an easy transition, but there are steps you can take to minimize the level of your pain and the length of time your grief lasts.

AFFIRMATION

I allow myself to experience the entire grief process.

EXERCISE

Take a few quiet moments and check in with your emotions to see if you can figure out where you are with your grief.

Can you think of reasons why you don't want to have your grief? Read the next five chapters on the stages of grief to increase your understanding of what each stage entails.

8

DENIAL

It's not denial. I'm just selective about the reality I accept.

~ Bill Watterson

Denial is the negating of reality. It comes upon us when something happens that goes against what we think should be happening or what we want to be happening. It's a normal reaction when something too painful occurs.

It's as if our brain goes into protection mode and shuts down. Amazingly, we see and hear only what we want to allow in. It is not a function of intelligence or will, rather it's a function of emotional readiness. It's also not conscious, meaning that it can happen without our awareness that it is happening.

Designed to help us integrate painful situations, the coping mechanism of denial helps us to avoid feeling a flood of intense emotions all at once; it helps us take things piece-meal. It is a healthy, normal, and vital part of the grief process. In fact, we need denial. The problems with denial occur when we cannot or will not move beyond it, when it continuously blinds us, or when we refuse to see and accept reality after the initial shock has passed.

Denial starts to cause problems when it won't allow a spouse to accept that the marriage is really over. For example, spouses in denial may badger their partners into staying, or they may drag their feet with the legal proceedings. Denial is normal early in the grief process, but if it continues for too long a time, it can be quite destructive.

Usually, a person who remains stuck in denial isn't getting adequate emotional support to accept the difficult situation. Seeking out supportive people (friends or other comforting people who also can be honest with you about what they see) or divorce professionals can help immensely when someone is stuck in this phase.

AFFIRMATION

My denial protects me until I no longer need protecting.

JOURNAL EXERCISE

- *Write about where you have been in denial about an aspect of your marriage or your divorce. How did you get out of denial? What resources helped you the most?*

- *Now write about where you may still be in denial. In facing your reality, what are you afraid of? What resources do you need to help you move from denial into the other stages of grief?*

9

ANGER

Anger is a great force. If you control it, it can be transmuted into a power which can move the whole world.

~ William Shenstone

Following denial, anger is the second stage in the grief process. It can be quite comforting to know and understand that anger is a normal part of dealing with a loss. Because many of us are taught that our anger is not okay (especially women), we may deny ourselves the very anger we need to move through the divorce.

Anger can serve as a powerful motivator for taking care of business; it comes from a strong place within us. When we feel angry, we are less likely to be or stay a victim and we are more apt to make change happen.

There are appropriate reasons to get angry and there are appropriate ways to express your anger. When anger is fresh, it is hardest to contain, which is why it's not usually good to say or do anything about your anger until you've calmed down.

However, stuffing your anger will have negative consequences for you because the ire doesn't go away. Instead, it festers and sometimes gets worse. Too much anger, like an excess of any emotion, can have diminishing returns. Rather than help you, it can begin to get in the way of your recovery process.

Ways to manage your anger in a healthy manner include talking with friends or professionals, journaling, or reading inspirational material.

Another important factor in dealing with anger is to understand whom you are angry with. So often, fingers are pointed outwardly toward your spouse, your family, your friends, or your bosses when, in reality, you are angry with yourself.

Perhaps you accepted abuse or turned your head in denial when there was clear evidence of a problem. Or maybe you regret your choices or feel you stayed too long and "wasted" all of your "good years."

If you don't get to the real root of your anger, you will not get to a deeper healing. It's like having an itch on your back and scratching your arm. You haven't reached the real problem until you acknowledge the ways in which you are upset with yourself.

AFFIRMATION

I allow myself to feel angry. I express my anger appropriately. I am learning from my mistakes and I am healing deeply and completely.

JOURNAL EXERCISE

- *Write about people other than yourself whom you feel anger toward: whom are you mad at and why?*

- *Next write a list of the ways in which you feel disappointed in or mad at yourself.*

- *Are any of the items on these two lists the same?*

- *What do you feel you have learned as a result of errors you have made?*

- *What do you need in order to heal from this experience?*

EXERCISE

There may be actions you can take, such as getting some exercise, going out into nature, or doing some type of creative endeavor that can help you to process your anger. Examples include listening to music, playing music, dancing, creating something with clay, doing any kind of artwork, going for a walk, or going for a drive.

10

BARGAINING

Never regret. If it's good, it's wonderful. If it's bad, it's experience.

~ Victoria Holt

Bargaining is probably the most elusive stage of the grief process, because most people do it without knowing that they are doing it. Bargaining comes from having the hope that things might turn out differently or from having regrets about what has gone wrong in the marriage and wishing you could have a second chance—a do-over, if you will. It is reflecting on what happened between you and your spouse, and then thinking over and over again what could or should have been different with you, your spouse, your kids, or a choice that was made, to name just a few possibilities.

Like the other four stages of grief, bargaining is a normal phase that you shouldn't necessarily try to avoid, but it is a phase that, left unchecked, can continue occurring for years after your divorce. It's important to recognize when you are bargaining so that you can learn how to work with it.

Anytime you find yourself thinking about what might have been or wishing things could have been different, you are bargaining with your past. Furthermore, if you are bargaining with what you might be able to make happen, you are bargaining with your future.

In some cases, it's healthy to revisit your decision in order to make sure a breakup is really what you both want and need. Some couples actually do get back together and make a renewed commitment to work on their relationship.

In other cases, too much bargaining or wishful thinking may be a sign of denial. This is why it's important to move through the bargaining phase, and if you find you are unable to, it is an indication that you need more mental and emotional support than you are getting.

AFFIRMATION

I accept reality. I do not regret the past.

JOURNAL EXERCISE

- *Keep a logbook with you at all times. Write down recurring thoughts you catch yourself having, like, "If I had only done X in my marriage, we wouldn't be divorcing," or "Why couldn't we have seen Y?"*

or "Maybe if I change how I feel about a particular behavior, we can work things out." These are all bargaining thoughts.

EXERCISE

If there is a thought you have repeatedly that you can't seem to shake, you may want to seek advice from a friend or divorce professional in order to process it thoroughly.

11

DEPRESSION

The walls we build around us to keep sadness out also keep out the joy.

~ Jim Rohn

Depression, which is probably the most uncomfortable of the five grief stages, can be debilitating. However, depression is not only a normal reaction to a divorce, it is also a healthy one. Anyone who doesn't feel some sadness after this type of loss (even when everyone involved sees it as a change for the better) was either not committed to the marriage in the first place, or not in touch with his or her emotions.

People often try to avoid feeling deep sadness, and when they do feel it, they try to control how long it lasts. One of the most difficult aspects of grieving in general and depression in particular is not knowing how long it will last. I often hear people say, "I should be over this by now."

But it doesn't work that way. The depression is over when it's over, not when you feel you've had enough. It will pass, but at times it can feel like an eternity. Understanding that depression is a necessary part of healing can help you stay with the discomfort.

Also, it's not uncommon to start feeling better and then get kicked right back into depression after running into an old friend, hearing "your" song on the radio, or noticing the passing of your anniversary. When this happens, it doesn't mean that anything is wrong, it simply indicates that you're not done feeling the sadness. Be gentle with yourself.

If you are tempted to distract yourself or to make yourself feel better, keep in mind that the degree to which you won't allow yourself to feel your sadness is the same degree to which you cut yourself off from feeling all emotions. Not only that, but you are simply prolonging the inevitable. These deep emotions of sadness need to be felt in order to pass.

AFFIRMATION

I allow myself to sit with the difficult feelings of sadness and depression, knowing that this is an integral part of my grief process.

JOURNAL EXERCISE

- *When you feel depressed, find a quiet place to write in your journal about what you are feeling and why. If it seems helpful, you can write the reason for your depression on a piece of paper and then tear the paper into small pieces. This can help you to let go.*

33

EXERCISE

If and when you feel ready, you can hold a burial service for your marriage. Here's one idea for setting up such a ritual:

1. *Gather together any photos you have of you and your spouse, small gifts, or anything else that reminds you of your spouse that you are ready to let go of.*

2. *Dig a hole in the ground approximately 2 feet deep and 2 feet wide. You can vary the size depending on your need. (You may be tempted to have someone else dig the hole for you, but it's important to dig it yourself, because digging is a part of what makes this ritual such a cathartic process.) Save the dirt you dig up for the next step.*

3. *Place all of the items you gathered into the hole you dug, say a prayer over them if you'd like, thank these memories for being a part of your life, and then cover them up with all the dirt you dug up.*

4. *Plant some forget-me-not seeds or your favorite flower or plant.*

This can be a symbolically powerful exercise to help you move through your grief process.

12

ACCEPTANCE

When one door closes, another opens; but we often look so long and so regretfully upon the closed door that we do not see the one which has opened for us.

~ Alexander Graham Bell

Loss can sometimes bring appreciation for what you had. Perhaps there were traits about your spouse or traditions you shared that you find hard to let go of in your divorce. I've often heard people say, "He's the only one who gets my sense of humor," or "I'll never find anyone who matches me on so many levels."

It can be painfully challenging to have to let go of a person or a marriage that had so many good aspects. Your inclination may be to focus on only the loss of those aspects and to forget the not-so-good parts of the relationship. The fear that we will never find what we once had may be pervasive.

Certainly, the connection you shared with your spouse can never be matched in exactly the same way, but if the trait you loved was in your spouse, it probably exists in someone else as well. Mourning the loss of the person you married, exchanged vows with, and perhaps had children with is entirely appropriate. The question is this: how long is too long to continue grieving?

Although there is no exact formula for how long grief should take (and grieving is a very personal process), there does come a point when you should be moving on—but you're stuck. That point may be more apparent to others than it is to you, but most people have a small voice within that tells them when it's time to move on.

Questions like "Why?" "Why me?" "Why now?" are futile because they don't change the reality of your situation and they prevent you from moving into the next chapter of your life.

AFFIRMATION

I will accept the conditions of my life today and move on.

JOURNAL EXERCISE

- *If you are feeling stuck in some aspect of your grief process, write about this aspect. Where are you stuck? Why do you believe you are stuck? What can you do to become more accepting and to move on?*

EXERCISE

If you're not sure whether or not you are stuck but you feel that you're not moving through your grieving process, ask a trusted friend or therapist to give you honest feedback about where they believe you are in your process.

It could be that you are not stuck but that you're not moving through your grief as quickly as you'd like. If this is the feedback you receive, it will be important to allow yourself more time and space to grieve.

13

ROLLER-COASTER RIDE

Feelings are much like waves, we can't stop them from coming but we can choose which one to surf.

~Jonatan Martensson

In this tumultuous time of financial, legal, and familial upheaval, you may experience many different (and extreme) emotions simultaneously. You may feel as though you are all over the emotional map and that your feelings have a life of their own—with you at their mercy. Some people going through divorce have told me they think they are "losing it," because they are experiencing so many new and intense emotions that their lives feel out of control.

The process of divorce can be much like riding a roller coaster. There are so many emotional highs and lows, and just when you think things are calming down and the ride is over, you get thrown for another loop.

Be patient, fasten your seatbelt, and expect the unexpected.

If you know that the ride will be long and bumpy, you are less likely to be upset when life takes you down instead of up or left instead of right. Get some support and go with the flow. Although this is good advice at anytime in life, it is especially true during the ending of a marriage and the changing of a family unit.

It may also help you to remember that life will eventually calm down again and you will return to a sense of normalcy. It might just take a while.

AFFIRMATION

I am patient on this roller-coaster ride. I wait for things to calm down, knowing that I can't rush the process.

JOURNAL EXERCISE

■ *Write about some intense emotions or experiences you've had. What have you done to get through these trying times? Is there anything from what you've done in the past that you can apply to your current situation?*

14

EMBRACING PAIN

We must embrace pain and burn it as fuel for our journey.

~ Kenji Miyazawa

Pain is an indication that something is wrong. Whatever the source of the pain is, whether physical or emotional, there is a wound that needs to be healed.

We are bombarded daily by the media with messages about pills, potions, and cures for our aches and pains. Overtly and covertly we are taught that there are quick, easy, and inexpensive ways to get rid of pain or discomfort. However, these quick fixes are usually designed to cover the pain temporarily; they are not meant to address the root of the problem or to heal the wound on a deeper level.

As a result of our believing these messages, many of us have lost our tolerance for all pain, including the pain we need to feel in order to grieve thoroughly.

Unless there is something quite extraordinary about you or your situation, you will not get through your divorce without feeling the pain that comes with the grief process. Pain is part of letting go of an important relationship that was once such a big part of your life. You must allow yourself to have your time to hurt.

Unacknowledged feelings don't go away—they linger. If you try to push your pain away, you will actually prolong your grieving process. Even though you may not like living with your uncomfortable feelings, by allowing yourself to fully feel your grief, you deepen as a person. Once healed and on the other side of your intense emotions, you'll likely find that you will have become a stronger person.

AFFIRMATION

I allow myself to feel the pain of this divorce knowing that it will pass when I am fully healed and that it will deepen and strengthen me.

JOURNAL EXERCISE

- *Make a list of the ways you try to diminish your pain (for example, by eating, sleeping, exercising, drinking, spending money, overworking, getting into new relationships, focusing on kids or others, or watching TV).*

■ *What are you afraid will happen if you allow yourself to hurt? What are you willing to do to stop running from your pain so you can acknowledge it and thus heal from it?*

■ *What resources do you need to support you at your most painful times?*

MEDITATION

Find a comfortable, quiet spot where you will not be disturbed. Then take three or four very deep breaths and allow whatever feelings you don't want to feel to come up and simply be with them. If you don't experience the emotion surfacing the first time you do this, don't be surprised. Just keep checking in with yourself and, as often as you can, do this meditation. Eventually, your deep emotions will present themselves and your healing will begin.

15

COURAGE

Courage isn't the absence of fear, but rather the judgment that something else is more important than fear.

~ Ambrose Redmoon

It takes courage to admit something is wrong and to work on repairing a marriage, and it takes courage to get divorced when it can't be repaired, especially when other people's lives, such as those of the children, relatives, and friends, are strongly impacted by the breakup. Furthermore, adjusting to a breakup that perhaps you didn't want and wouldn't choose also takes courage.

Webster defines courage as the mental or moral strength to venture, persevere, or withstand danger, fear, or difficulty. So much else in life requires courage, but a major transition such as divorce may require all the courage you've got and then some.

Standing up for yourself is tougher than going along with the crowd. Moving on from a hurtful event or a bad relationship is harder than staying stuck in unhappiness or living a lie. Seeing things clearly and taking action take more courage than ignoring problems and putting blinders on. Every time we stay in situations that are not good for us because we are too afraid to leave, we suffer. When we cling to an unhealthy known because we are afraid to deal with unknowns, we suffer.

Breaking through fear and comfort to create a new life for yourself requires a great deal of courage. Remember that fear is a normal part of any change; what is important at this time is first allowing yourself to feel your fear and then taking the next step to move through your marriage's dissolution as best you can, with courage.

AFFIRMATION

I will move through my divorce with courage.

JOURNAL EXERCISE

- *Write down descriptions of three to five events in your life when you felt fear but took an action anyway. What did you learn about yourself from those experiences?*

- *Now write about three to five fears you are currently facing. What can you apply from your previous experiences to your current situation about how to move through fear?*

MEDITATION

Think for a moment about a fear you have today. Without going too deeply into why you are afraid, imagine yourself moving through this situation with strength, ease, and courage.

16

CHARACTER

Adversity does not build character. Adversity reveals character.

~ Sandra Dahl, widow of
Joseph Dahl, captain of United Airlines
Flight 93 on September 11, 2001

Webster defines character as moral excellence and firmness. Morals provide us with our sense of what is right and what is wrong. Having a good character would then mean not only knowing the right thing to do but doing it.

When faced with a challenge that brings out the worst in you (for example, your most fear-based thinking, your most intense anger or jealousy, your greatest sense of having been wronged), your character is truly tested. Dividing assets and debts, determining arrangements for child custody and support, learning how to coparent, and deciding who gets to keep the house are just a few examples of the tremendous tasks you may be facing currently.

If you are angry, will you give in to your lower self, the part of you that wants to get even, the part that says, "I'll show him" (or her), the part that wants to manipulate another for your personal gain? Or will you call on your higher self, that aspect of your self that sees the big picture and keeps the best interest of the children, or working to maintain a good relationship with your spouse, at the top of the priority list? If you feel cheated, can you give more than you get, can you let go of feeling wronged, or will you want your spouse to pay financially and emotionally for the pain you are suffering?

You are only human and, as such, you may have your bad days. You will probably make mistakes and act compulsively. You may say and do things during your divorce process that you will later regret. The way to build character and maintain your integrity through this greatly challenging time is to keep aspiring to act from your higher, more mature self. When you do act from your lower self, be aware of that and apologize immediately, even when your lower self thought your spouse deserved the comment or action.

AFFIRMATION

I will strive to act from my higher self each and every day throughout my divorce process.

JOURNAL EXERCISE

- *Make a list of times during your divorce that you acted from your lower self and of times when you acted from your higher self. For each incident, what resulted from your actions/comments? Did the interaction turn out positively or negatively?*

- *If it was negative, what could you have done to turn the situation around? If it was positive, what happened to change the negative dynamic?*

- *Write about what you learned from these interactions.*

17

A BETTER DIVORCE

Every one of us alone has the power to direct the course of our lives by choosing what actions we will or won't take. While sometimes it's easier to believe you don't have a choice, the reality is that you always have a choice to behave differently.

~ Francine Ward

When we hear the word "divorce," most of us conjure up the image of two people engaged in a battle over child custody, child or spousal support, and the division of assets. Traditionally, each side had its respective attorney, whose job was to duke it out with the other side in an effort to win the best settlement possible. Then, once the divorce was over and done with, the ex-spouses were so angry with each other that they remained enemies.

Although contentious litigation is still the preferred method for many divorcing people, the good news is that there are many alternatives to this type of divorce.

Even if your spouse (or ex-spouse) is behaving badly, you don't have to follow suit. You can have what's referred to as a "good divorce" or as a "better divorce." To do this, however, you must be willing to handle yourself in a mature manner, which I refer to as your "higher self." This is not always easy to do, especially when you may have fears about your sense of security running rampant through your brain, or when your spouse has done something you feel is flagrantly unjust.

This is not to say that you shouldn't feel your feelings. Indeed you should. What this passage refers to is controlling your behavior: that is, can you be incredibly angry with your spouse and not seek vengeance by way of unethical behavior in the divorce settlement? Can you, instead, express yourself calmly and save your heated emotions for another forum, such as your therapist's office or hitting a punching bag at the gym? Can you soothe yourself in a healthy way?

If you've never done this, it will undoubtedly be a tall task to begin conducting yourself this way through your divorce proceedings, but you will likely feel better once you get to the other side.

One trick to help you control your reactions to events during your divorce is to not speak in the moment. If your spouse says or does something hurtful, you can bite your tongue, walk away, hang up the phone, or say, "I can't answer that right now. Let me think about it." This is a way to respond rather than react.

Some couples who have contentious relationships prefer communicating by e-mail so they don't have to speak to their ex-spouses. They can take a few deep breaths and reply only when they are ready. Some people use another trick: depersonalizing their spouses' actions, which means not taking personally anything their spouses say or do, and seeing the problem as a part of their spouses' shortcomings, not theirs.

Although, in the moment, it can sometimes feel delicious to send a sharp barb your spouse's way or have what feels like a victory, the reality is that divorce doesn't have to be a train wreck that leaves a mess of ashes and ruined fragments behind for you and your children. A divorce can be done in a mature, healthy way that minimizes pain and anger. Let it start with you.

AFFIRMATION

I act from my higher self through my divorce and afterward.

JOURNAL EXERCISE

- *Write down how you normally act when your spouse makes you angry. Do you make mean comments to other people? Do you throw things? Do you yell and scream?*

- *Now write down some alternative ways to behave that you think would be acting from your higher self. Begin putting these new ways into practice and see what happens.*

51

18

YOUR OWN PACE

Quiet minds cannot be perplexed or frightened but go on in fortune or misfortune at their own private pace, like a clock during a thunderstorm.

~ Robert Louis Stevenson

The rate at which your divorce (and, for that matter, your divorce recovery) proceeds is an important factor that most people don't consider until they are well into the process. But one day, you may begin to feel that matters are going too slowly or too quickly or you may notice that your spouse is trying to move faster or slower than what you are comfortable with. This is the pacing of the process, and each person has his or her own sense of timing.

Certain key factors determine your pace: whether or not the decision to divorce was mutual; whether the decision was sudden or well thought-out; and what your two personalities and temperaments are like.

In the event that you both saw the breakup coming, it's likely that you can get through the dissolution relatively quickly. There will be fewer hitches and, since the decision to split is mutual, you and your spouse are likely to agree on more issues. You are also likely to move on from your marriage more quickly.

However, when one spouse wants the marriage to end and the other doesn't, the spouse who wants to save the marriage often takes significantly longer to get through the financial and legal process because they are still trying to integrate the marital dissolution mentally and emotionally.

If there was an element of surprise involved in which one spouse sprung the news of the desired divorce on the other, it can take months for the initial shock and denial to wear off, which can slow the process down considerably.

If you were the initiator of the divorce, you may want things to go faster so you can begin your new life. On the other hand, if your spouse is leaving you (even if it isn't a surprise), you will likely be moving more slowly, as you accept the decision your spouse made to end the marriage.

Or perhaps the patterns of your divorce process will resemble the patterns of your marriage—one of you may have always done things slowly and methodically and the other always wanted everything to happen more quickly.

Being prepared for these pacing differences can change the expectations you have for one another to either "get things done" or to "stop pushing!" This holds true in many areas of your life, but it can be particularly pronounced during a marital dissolution.

AFFIRMATION

I acknowledge my own pace as well as that of my spouse. We continually work together to find a pace that is acceptable to both of us.

JOURNAL EXERCISE

- *Where do you see yourself in the divorce process? Write about your perfect pace.*

- *Where do you see your spouse? What do you think your spouse's perfect pace is?*

- *What would compromise look and feel like?*

- *Is there a conversation you can have with your spouse about timing? What would you say? Write out an imaginary conversation with your spouse about timing.*

19

DON'T BELIEVE EVERYTHING YOU THINK

I am an old man and have known a great many troubles,
but most of them never happened.

~ Mark Twain

As you proceed through the divorce process, you may be tempted to think about all the bad things that can happen. You may have already spent a great deal of energy inventing worst-case scenarios in order to feel more in control of your situation. For example, you may have thought something like this: "If I can think of all the bad things that could happen, I will be better prepared when they do happen."

In reality, thinking these thoughts doesn't create one bit more control over your situation. The only result that can come from such imaginings is that you will feel even more tired and depleted than you already do just from dealing with all that actually comes with your divorce.

There is so much in life we have no control over, but the good news is that you do have control over what you think. You can stop dwelling on the bad things anytime you choose to, and you will free up precious energy that you need for other tasks. All it takes is the mental discipline to keep your mind focused on the present moment and to stop going into a negative mind-set. Note that mental discipline gets easier with practice.

Given that you are making up stories when you imagine worst-case scenarios, why not make up a story that makes you feel good, the best-case scenario? It has an equal probability of occurring. As a result of changing your thoughts, you will feel better and have more energy to meet the real challenges directly in front of you.

AFFIRMATION

I need only to focus on my current reality as I go through my divorce process.

JOURNAL EXERCISE

■ *Write down some of the worst-case scenarios that you fear might happen as a result of your divorce. Sometimes it can help to get them out of your head and onto paper.*

- *Now write a story that would be the opposite outcome or what you would consider to be the best-case scenario.*

- *Which one makes you feel better to think about?*

MEDITATION

Set a timer for five minutes, find a comfortable place to sit and think about a story that makes you feel better.

20

CHALLENGES AND GIFTS

The web of our life is of a mingled yarn, good and ill together....

~ William Shakespeare

With every gift, there is a challenge, and with every challenge, there is a gift. Even though divorce may be one of the greatest challenges you will ever have to face, there will be gifts in it along the way. It may be hard to imagine those gifts from where you sit now, but in every aspect of life there is no good without some bad or bad without some good.

The gifts often arrive in the most unexpected or unimaginable ways. Even events that initially appear to be bad can turn into gifts.

Perhaps, as a result of your changing life, you've met some wonderful people or deepened some important relationships, you've found a new favorite walking path or bookstore, or some friends sold you their car at a bargain price because they knew you couldn't afford it otherwise.

Perhaps you've had to move, return to work, take your kids from their old school and put them in a new school. Or maybe you've had to learn to live as a single person again. These are all events that you may feel are intrinsically bad because you would not have chosen to live this way or do this thing.

But then you realize that you're able to create your own new home, you like having to work and your new job is better than your old one, your kids are learning how to make new friends, and you are more self-reliant than you ever knew you were. Out of all these challenges, some good resulted.

Be open to the idea that something good will happen.

Through your divorce, and possibly as a result of it, you will grow in ways that you couldn't or wouldn't if you were still working on repairing your marriage.

If you haven't experienced the new growth or recognized the gifts yet, give it time. When you've moved some distance away from the pain, you may see that some old wounds have healed, some places that were weak are stronger now, and you've learned some important life lessons. These are all gifts.

AFFIRMATION

I trust that through this tremendous challenge, I will continue to face the challenges and look for the gifts.

JOURNAL EXERCISE

■ *Make a list of five to ten negative events you've had to
 contend with as a result of your divorce process. List
 the events and describe why they were negative.*

■ *Now look at your list and write down the positive
 effects that have come as a result. If you can't think
 of anything positive, leave a blank space next to the
 event and revisit your list every month for the next
 year or until you see that you, your kids, or your
 family did benefit from this event.*

■ *If you get stuck and simply can't find anything positive to say about the event, ask a friend to give you
 some thoughts on it. Sometimes, we get so invested
 in seeing something as bad or wrong that we become
 blind to seeing it any other way.*

21

SHOWING UP

Hope begins in the dark, the stubborn hope that if you just show up and try to do the right thing, the dawn will come. You wait and watch and work: you don't give up.

~ Anne Lamott

One of the most challenging aspects of divorce is to show up day after day for what sometimes feels like a never-ending negative experience. It takes energy to stay with the process and a willingness to keep going, even when you have no idea where you will end up.

You will have moments when you will be tempted to throw in the towel and give up. It's important not to give in to this thought or desire. You may be required to muster all the inner strength you have and then some, but it is very important that you show up.

Most people can endure challenging times day by day, and piece by piece, but if they had to deal with the challenges all at once, they would burn out.

Imagine that you are standing at the bottom of a very steep hill. If you look up, the climb will seem daunting. My advice is this: Don't look up! Keep your eyes on the road right in front of you and you will be more capable of climbing to the top of the hill.

Thinking about everything you need to do to get to the top will make the trip seem impossible, but giving yourself fully to this moment and taking one action is something you can do.

AFFIRMATION

I show up for each task in front of me.

JOURNAL EXERCISE

- *Using the hill analogy above, make a list of all the things you see ahead of you in your divorce process that will need your attention. For these tasks or events, write the number 3 next to anything that will need more than six months to complete or that will be completed by someone other than yourself—that is, your spouse or your attorney.*

- *Next, write the number 2 next to any task that will take longer than two weeks to accomplish but will take fewer than six months.*

- *Finally, write the number 1 next to any task or event that will be coming up in the next two weeks. These are the tasks that need your attention now.*

Although there may be times you need to plan for or to focus on those tasks that are not immediate, this exercise will help you to take your divorce process piece by piece. This is an exercise that you can complete anytime you are feeling overwhelmed with all that needs to be done.

22

MAKING PROMISES

The best way to keep one's word is not to give it.

~ Napoleon

Marital dissolution is a time of major transition in almost every area of your life, your spouse's life, and the lives of your children. Many aspects of life will be changing for all of you. Because you may feel protective of others or responsible (that is, you may not have "had to" divorce, or perhaps you initiated the split), you may want everyone to feel reassured that it will all work out. But in your attempts to be reassuring, you may make promises you have no business making.

The reason you shouldn't make such promises is that you don't have all the facts, and when your life is in so much flux, you don't know what the future holds. The best course to take is to not make any promises at all, even if it means that others are left hanging or that they don't get the answers they want and may need.

Examples of how you might carelessly give your word occur when you say things like, "I won't ask for the house in the divorce settlement," or "No, kids, you won't have to change schools." Then when you get new information that causes you to change your mind, you either have to go back on your word or forego something that is important to you.

Often, spouses will try to sit down and negotiate the terms of the settlement. This is not a bad practice; in fact, I recommend talking about what assets and debts you have if you can. Just don't promise anything, one way or another.

If you feel pressured, a great thing to say is, "I just need more time to think about this" or "I want to consult my divorce professional before I respond one way or another." And you can say to your children, "I don't know for sure what's going to happen, but I will do all I can to keep you in the same school. If anything changes, I'll let you know as soon as I can, so there won't be any surprises."

A good practice to follow is not to give your word when you aren't sure that you'll be able to keep it, even when things calm down in your life. It is especially important not to make empty promises to yourself or to anyone else during your divorcing days.

AFFIRMATION

I won't make promises I can't keep today.

JOURNAL EXERCISE

- *Write down any ideas you have of things you would like to promise your spouse or your kids right now. Circle any of these promises that you've already said—or would like to say—to appease them, knowing that you can't really ensure that this promise will be kept.*

- *If there are any promises left uncircled (meaning you're sure you can deliver), write about why you are sure and how you will keep this promise.*

- *What did you learn by doing this exercise?*

23

NOTHING EXTRA

Do what you can, with what you have, where you are.

~ Theodore Roosevelt

During this tumultuous time in your life, you will be faced with many crossroads and many decisions. Having to make choices for anything can be stressful at anytime. When you are dissolving your marriage, the choices you must make may be especially difficult. For example, decisions about how to divide the assets, who should take care of the kids, and where you should live increase stress levels even more.

If there is anything you don't have to choose between, do, or decide for a while, then don't do anything about it. Take it off the table. You can always come back to it later, and it will be a big help to you to have one less item on your list to think about right now.

For those who are especially emotional during the divorce proceedings, it may be best to postpone all decisions—even those that seem most pressing—at least until you're feeling less stressed and less vulnerable. If a decision must be made within a specific time frame and you can't wait, I highly recommend seeking professional advice to resolve the matter.

With the additional stress divorce brings, everyday obligations, such as driving your kids to school, having to sit in rush-hour traffic and be at work by 8:00 a.m., or having to get a leaky faucet fixed can serve as the final straw that breaks the camel's back.

When you are stretched the way divorce can stretch you, ask for help and support. Simple changes, such as arranging carpooling with your neighbor, asking your boss for a two-month change of schedule until you get things figured out, or even letting the leaky faucet drip for another month can make a world of difference in finding your center and becoming grounded again.

When you are overly stressed by anything, you may not be as present while driving, walking, and working, which puts you and those around you at risk for health and safety problems. Do what you can to keep everything as simple as possible.

AFFIRMATION

When I feel stressed, I will slow down and ask for help when I need it. I will not make any decisions I don't have to make today.

JOURNAL EXERCISE

■ *Write a list of some of the tasks and choices you are dealing with right now. Cross off anything that you don't have to do. Then write a 3 next to those tasks or decisions that are low priority or that you can ask someone else to do; put a 2 next to anything that must be taken care of in the next two weeks; and finally, place a 1 beside those things that need more immediate attention (that is, there could severe consequences if you don't take care of these items).*

■ *Have someone check your list to be sure that you're not trying to take on too much.*

■ *Are there any items on your list that you need professional assistance with? If so, write down which items they are and whom you need to contact.*

■ *Having a list such as this can make your plan clearer and easier to follow. It can also provide you with some direction as you proceed. You may even want to ask a trusted friend to look over the list or help you determine who can do what, and by when it needs to get done.*

24

IF ONLY

One's real life is often the life that one does not lead.

~ Oscar Wilde

One of the most common thoughts people share when their marriage ends is the loss of the hope they once had. Ideas like these are often stated: "If only she'd gotten sober." "If only he could have stayed faithful." "If only the therapist could have reached him." "If only someone had intervened."

It's difficult to move on from such types of thoughts, especially when you feel that several relatively minor issues or just one major issue caused your marriage to fail.

One woman told me recently she had loved her husband and had wished only that he had been more mature. In her mind, their marriage could have worked if her husband had simply grown up and stopped acting like a bachelor. She seemed almost ready to blame her husband's therapist for the breakup by saying that she wished the therapist had been more direct with her husband.

Although I know that there are ways in which people can and do change, they transform only because they want to and are ready to—not because someone is forcing them to change or convincing them that they should view themselves and the world differently.

As frustrating as it may be, whether the issue causing conflict is the need for a partner to be more responsible or the need to end an addiction, you cannot force another person to change.

No matter how close you felt you were to having the partner you wanted, you did not have that partner. You left your spouse, or your spouse left you, or the breakup was mutual. In any of these three scenarios, neither you nor your partner had enough of what you wanted and needed from the other spouse, even if it missed by only a hair.

It will make your divorce experience much harder to endure if you continue to think about what a great relationship you could have had. "If only he had loved me more," or "If only she had wanted kids," or "If only he had stopped gambling." Whenever you find yourself feeling sad, depressed, hurt, or angry because of how it might have been, stop thinking those thoughts. Instead, remind yourself of the disappointments, embarrassments, hurt, and pain that were caused by what was missing. Whatever was missing in your relationship was significant, because if it hadn't been, you would have been able to save your marriage if both of you had wanted to change and had been able to change.

AFFIRMATION

I accept reality today and don't let myself dwell on "if only."

JOURNAL EXERCISE

- *Write out some of your "if only's" and leave some space after each one. In that space, write about what your real and entire experience in this area was.*

- *Could you have done anything differently or influenced your spouse (or the circumstances) to have created a different outcome?*

- *Do you believe that your marriage is over, or do you fantasize that you and your spouse will get back together? Write in your journal about this topic. Use the following questions to guide your writing.*

- *What aspects of your marriage and divorce do you find hard to accept.*

- *Why are these things so hard to come to terms with?*

- *What is preventing you from accepting things as they are?*

25

WHAT WILL PEOPLE THINK?

What people think of you is none of your business.

~ Author unknown

When divorcing people start telling friends and family about their impending split, one great worry they have is, "What will people think?" Fear of criticism and the judgment of others abounds.

The unfortunate truth is that there will be people who will look down their noses at you for divorcing or who will no longer want to associate with you; however, how people react is more about them and their shortcomings than it is about you and anything you might have done.

This is easy to remember when the person judging you is a neighbor down the street you don't care much for anyway, but when it's a parent, a sibling, or a close friend, it can be quite hard to deal with. We all want to feel approved of and accepted by those we care about.

Regardless of the role they may play in your life, if some people criticize you for your choice to divorce or the circumstances of your divorce, that is indicative of their insensitivity to your needs.

Often, those who judge divorcing people harshly are those who fear divorce becoming their own reality. Or they may resent the fact that divorce is a choice available to you but not to them; they have to suffer, why can't you?

You will cope much better with others' criticism and judgments if you can keep these facts in mind. It won't excuse the judgers' actions, but if you know that they are reacting from fear or anger at something that has nothing to do with you, that insight might help you to not take their reaction personally.

AFFIRMATION

I will not take personally the reactions others may have to my divorce.

JOURNAL EXERCISE

■ *Keep a log of those you tell about your divorce, and note the reaction each person has to your news. If there is a reaction that is particularly hurtful, you may have to make a decision as to whether you want that person to remain in your life. Similarly, if someone reacts in a way that feels especially supportive, it will also be good to note this so that you can ask others to provide similar support.*

26

DEEP PAIN

Love means exposing yourself to the pain of being hurt,
deeply hurt, by someone you trust.

~ Renita Weems

Going through a divorce can hurt so deeply that, at times, you feel as though you're being stretched further than you've ever been stretched before—mentally, emotionally, physically, and financially. If you have been through tough times in your life before, you may have the inner knowledge that you will survive this ordeal, but right now all you experience is your pain.

When a marriage ends, it's not just the pain of losing love that you endure. There's also the sadness at the loss of the dream of living happily ever after and the anger at being unable to trust in any kind of permanence. For some, the plain facts that caused the breakup of the marriage can also add layers of pain—for example, having been cheated on sexually, having had your spouse act irresponsibly with joint finances, or your spouse having had an addiction which, despite his or her love for you, couldn't be given up. This pain can be all-consuming.

While in the midst of such challenging periods, most of us feel these trying times will be our reality forever and ever; time seems to drag along endlessly. It's not uncommon for deep pain to cause depression, which can lead to a loss (or an increase) of appetite or sleep, apathy, or isolating behaviors.

If your pain reaches this level of suffering, it's important to seek out additional support from friends, family, and professionals.

Remember that your pain will eventually pass and you will feel whole again, and that pain is a necessary part of the grieving process. Someday you will look back and see how you grew as a result of going through such a painful experience.

AFFIRMATION

I will keep putting one foot in front of the other and ask for help when I need it, and I know that, eventually, the pain will subside.

JOURNAL EXERCISE

■ *Writing about your pain can help you acknowledge it as well as help you understand it. Keep a log of those times when you feel most sad, hurt, angry, lonely, or grief-stricken (or any other painful emotion).*

■ *Write about why you are feeling these feelings, and try to notice whether there are times when you are particularly susceptible to feeling bad.*

27

TEARS

There is a sacredness in tears. They are not the mark of weakness, but of power. They speak more eloquently than ten thousand tongues. They are messengers of overwhelming grief and unspeakable love.

~ Washington Irving

To cry at the loss of a loved one, a single nuclear family, or a dream, or at the injustices you may be experiencing in your marital dissolution is a healthy response to this life event. Having to divide as a couple or as a family is sad and painful even under the best of circumstances.

Crying is not a sign of weakness; it is a sign of being a sentient person. Those who try not to cry or not to feel sad do themselves a disservice on many levels.

Shedding tears is a way to cleanse the soul of grief and the pain of loss; it also provides physical benefits. Tears literally make you feel better by releasing toxins that would otherwise build up in your body. If you've ever had a "good cry," you know that after the crying ends, you actually feel more relaxed and calmer. Crying is a physical as well as an emotional release in that it slows down your heart rate and helps you to breathe a little deeper and more fully. It moves grief out of your cells. It is cathartic. (*Catharsis* can be defined as an event that produces a feeling of being purified emotionally, spiritually, or psychologically as a result of experiencing an intense emotional experience or a therapeutic technique.)

When you allow yourself to shed tears and truly grieve, you move through the grieving process faster than if you try to squelch your emotions in some way.

One way to think about this that may help is that every time you allow yourself to feel sad, you are that much closer to being on the other side of the pain. Shutting down your grief doesn't make it go away; rather it prevents you from moving through it. Your tears will flow when you are ready to cry and they will stop when you're done grieving.

AFFIRMATION

Today, I allow myself to cry whatever tears I need to cry.

JOURNAL EXERCISE

- *The action of writing can sometimes bring emotions to the surface so that you can feel them and express them. Then you can work on healing. If you are having a hard time getting in touch with your emotions, you may want to do some journaling in order to have this happen.*

- *There may be times when no matter what you do, you cannot uncover what you're feeling. In these instances, don't try to push it. Just allow yourself to get there when you get there.*

EXERCISE

If you feel the need to cry and you truly want to but you cannot cry, go to a sad movie (or rent one). Sad scenes can often trigger tears.

28

EXPECTATIONS

Anger always comes from frustrated expectations.

~ Elliott Larson

An expectation can be described as the way we think something should be, look, or turn out. Often, when things don't meet our expectations, we become upset. It's not wrong to have expectations, but they are subjective ideas based on how we were taught to treat others or on our past experience. Deciding how others should act, think, and feel can be very unfair to those on whom we place these expectations.

One common dynamic that reveals the respective expectations a husband and wife may have during the dissolution of their marriage is seen in coparenting situations. One parent may think that during or following a divorce, life should go on as usual and the kids should maintain their routines; the other parent, feeling bad about putting the children through this ordeal, may think the kids should have some extra-positive experiences to offset the negative fallout from the divorce.

Too often, what ends up happening is that each parent thinks the other parent's approach is wrong. They get angry with each other and then they begin working against each other.

Since not everyone shares the same ideas and assumptions about how such matters should be handled, it can be invaluable to try to understand the other spouse's perspective, instead of jumping to the conclusion that he or she is wrong. If you let go of your expectations and try harder to understand the other person's perspective, the interaction might change completely from contentious to cooperative.

If each spouse sincerely asked the other why he or she is doing whatever he or she is doing, it could increase each person's understanding of the other. When you understand each other, you are more likely to try to meet in the middle. Perhaps you will take turns with the routines, as well as with special events, so the coparenting dynamics will become more balanced and amicable.

Certainly, this is easier said than done; but it takes only one person to change a negative dynamic to a positive one.

AFFIRMATION

I release my expectations for the purpose of working cooperatively with my spouse.

JOURNAL EXERCISE

- *Write down the ways in which you and your spouse currently work at cross-purposes with each other. Why do you think this is so? What would you like your spouse to know about your perspective? Can you ask your spouse his or her perspective on the issue?*

- *How can you change your expectations or keep them in check so as not to impose them on your spouse?*

29

PATIENCE

*Have patience with all things, but chiefly have patience
with yourself. Do not lose courage in considering your
own imperfections, but instantly set about remedying
them—every day begin the task anew.*

~ Saint Francis de Sales

Make a conscious commitment to yourself to be patient,
loving, and kind to yourself today and throughout your
divorce process. Being upset with yourself depletes some of
the energy that you may need for other tasks on your dissolution journey.

Imagine that your energy, time, and resources are pieces
of a pie. In any given day, there are certain things you must
get done, but you have only so many slices in your "pie" to dole
out; it is finite. As you go through the stages of your divorce,
you may find that your pie is smaller than you thought it was.
This can be disconcerting, but it is not uncommon.

Most divorcing people will experience intense emotions; be called upon to make several major decisions (some of which may have an impact on them for years to come); and undergo many changes in lifestyle. All of these aspects of divorce can be energy-draining.

Expecting yourself to function at 100 percent while you are divorcing is both unrealistic and unfair. If you don't allow for the possibility that you may feel overwhelmed, exhausted, or just purely emotional on some days, you are setting yourself up to be disappointed in yourself, at best.

You can't be, do, or give more than you already have, particularly now. Remember that all of the divorce-related tasks will get done in due time. Things will fall into place in their own time. You can't force solutions. And you can't do it all alone.

Learn to be patient and to ask for help. Slow down, breathe, and allow yourself to be the limited human being that you are.

AFFIRMATION

I am patient and gentle with myself throughout my divorce process.

JOURNAL EXERCISE

- *Just before bedtime, think about the day that just ended. Were you impatient or upset with yourself for any reason? If so, what was the cause?*

- *If you were hard on yourself in the past twenty-four hours, write about how you can be gentler with yourself, given all that you are asked to do.*

- *Make a list of tasks you have ahead of you. Place a number next to each task in the order of their priority. Which tasks will have the greatest impact on your life now or in the future? Which things must get done sooner rather than later?*

- *It may help to write out a time line for these tasks and then ask a friend, attorney, or counselor to read it in order to judge whether you are being realistic or expecting too much of yourself.*

30

DISPOSITION

I've learned from experience that the greater part of our happiness or misery depends on our dispositions, not on our circumstances.

~ Martha Washington

In any life situation that is not to your liking, you can see yourself as a victim or you can see the situation as a challenge; you can approach it with apathy or with enthusiasm. You don't always have a choice as to what cards life deals you, but you do have a choice in how you view what is happening to you.

Much of our culture (as well as many other cultures around the world) view divorce as a failure. Divorce is considered a negative life event and one that most people wish they didn't have to endure. It represents loss on many levels, and it is often tremendously difficult and expensive to get through.

Divorce may never be an event that societies endorse, but it absolutely does not need to be looked upon as failure.

Nor does it need to be experienced in a "War of the Roses" manner, in which families are torn to shreds. It is a passage: the closing of one chapter and the beginning of another.

If you can trust that everything happens for a reason and learn to look for the good in all things, it may not make the difficult tasks easy, but it will make your experience better.

This is a tall order, especially if you didn't want the marriage to end, but it is an important skill to begin building. As you move through this transition, it will likely get easier to recognize the positive aspects of the experience, your spouse, and yourself, and to begin to feel better about divorce.

AFFIRMATION

I will focus on seeing things in a more positive light today.

JOURNAL EXERCISE

- *Write down some things that have occurred recently that you see as negative events.*

- *Practice looking for the good by writing something positive about one of these events. For example, "I've had to drastically downsize as a result of the divorce. Life is simpler, there's not as much to clean. It's my own space, in which I will get stronger and will recuperate from all I've been through."*

■ *Next, write a gratitude list about the event. Your list might look something like this:*

■ I'm grateful that I have a place to live.

■ I'm grateful that I'm far away from the tensions of my troubled marriage.

■ I'm grateful for the friends who helped me to move.

■ I'm grateful that my living situation is taken care of so I can focus on other things.

31

LIMITED VISIBILITY

It's like driving a car at night. You never see further than your headlights but you can make the whole trip that way.

~ E. L. Doctorow

As you navigate the divorce process, having limited visibility can be quite disconcerting. The experience can feel as if you're groping in the dark, and because you can't see down the entire length of the road, you may feel as though you'll surely lose your way.

It's challenging not to know exactly where you are headed. In order to feel more in control of your situation, you may try to rush the process in the hopes that you can see around the next corner sooner. Or you may be tempted to stop the process and look for an exit ramp. For many people going through a divorce, these are natural impulses. Yet more often than not, such attempts at having a greater sense of control prove futile and may even create additional chaos.

Remember that during your divorce process you don't necessarily have to see how the whole journey will unfold all the way through to the journey's end. Just keep your eyes on the road directly in front of you, and keep on keeping on. You will reach the end point in due time, and the way will be made clearer. Be patient.

AFFIRMATION

I keep my eyes on the path directly ahead of me and I know that the way will be made clear to me as I go.

JOURNAL EXERCISE

- *List some areas in your divorce process where you've felt frustrated at not knowing more. Is there anything you can do to improve your ability to see the whole process? If not, describe some other ways to make yourself feel better, such as learning to place more trust in the professionals you've hired, trusting your own instincts, and maintaining a comfortable pace with the proceedings (as much as you are able to, because your spouse has some say in this matter as well).*

MEDITATION

Get comfortably seated in a place where you will not be disturbed, and close your eyes. Then, imagine that you are driving at night on a winding road with your high beams on. As you drive, you see that you are headed into the light of dawn, and the road ahead of you is gradually becoming illuminated. Soon you will be able to see so much more. Knowing this, drive slowly to take in all of the beauty, sit back, relax, and simply be where you are.

32

THE ENEMY INSIDE

It is hard to fight an enemy who has outposts in your head.

~ Sally Kempton

Being your own worst enemy and engaging in negative self-talk is never helpful, and it can be especially destructive during a major life transition, such as a divorce.

You may tell yourself you shouldn't have left or that you shouldn't have left when you did. Or if your spouse left you, you may be reliving everything you think you did wrong during your marriage, or you might be putting yourself down for not having been a better spouse.

There is an important distinction you must make between looking at your part in why your marriage ended and beating yourself up because things didn't work out. Taking responsibility for your part in the relationship's demise is a sign of emotional maturity.

By examining your part, you can make important changes in yourself that will benefit any future relationships you will have. It is a constructive act.

On the other hand, being hard on yourself and telling yourself all the things you did wrong doesn't serve anyone. It doesn't bring change, and it makes you (and perhaps others) feel bad. It is a destructive act.

You are human, therefore you have regrets. Now or sometime in the future, you will have the benefit of hindsight to see how you could have been a better spouse or how you could have handled some situations more amicably. It may become obvious that you "should have" chosen a different path when you were given a particular life choice.

We all have regrets, but to focus on them and punish yourself for being human will not change what has already come to pass. When moving forward, the important task is to learn what you can from your past and then apply that wisdom to the choices in front of you.

AFFIRMATION

I will focus on having only constructive thoughts about my marriage and myself.

JOURNAL EXERCISE

- *Write down some of the negative self-talk in your mind. For example,* "I should never have let my spouse handle all of the finances. I'm so stupid. What was I thinking?"

- *Next, write out why you believe you made that choice.* "I made the choice to let him handle the money because he is better at budgets than I am." Or "I turned the finances over to her because she likes to take care of bills and I hate it."

- *Then write what you learned.* "I've learned that I must know and understand my own household finances."

- *Finally, write out what you will commit to do differently in the future:* "I will make sure I know what is happening with my money and, even if I don't deal with it directly, I will keep track of my finances."

33

DIVORCE THROUGH DIFFERENT LENSES

Every [person] takes the limits of his own field of vision for the limits of the world.

~ Arthur Schopenhauer

People are sometimes deeply hurt or angered by their perceptions of how their spouse is dealing with the divorce. They may see their spouse as coldhearted or too emotional, or they may feel hurt that their spouse seems to be moving on so quickly, or contrarily, they may feel frustrated that their spouse isn't cooperating with the divorce process.

There are numerous factors that affect how people act and react throughout the divorce process. Sometimes taking the time to understand the other person's perspective can make a world of difference in terms of expectations and judgments of the other.

Here are two such factors that stand out: (1) whether there is a "leaver" and a "leavee" (note that when the decision to divorce is arrived at mutually, the couple often sees matters from more similar vantage points) and (2) the gender differences between men and women.

By and large, leavers tend to feel more guilt for wanting to end the marriage. However, if they have already been through their grief stages during the marriage, when divorce proceedings begin, they are ready to move on. This can be very hard for the leavee, who often feels a sense of shock and betrayal and is slower to acknowledge that the divorce is really happening.

This perspective may explain why leavees sometimes feel so replaceable when their partners move on, and why leavers get so angry when they feel their spouses aren't cooperating. Certainly, there are cases where one spouse purposely tries to hurt the other, but in most cases, the main factor in one's ability to move through a divorce has more to do with one's emotional and mental state than with being malicious or ill-willed.

The other distinction worth examining is the difference in the ways that men and women deal with their divorces. These differences are due both to societal norms and physiology. Men and women are "wired" differently. Generally speaking, men are better able to compartmentalize their lives. This is why they may sometimes appear to be emotionless as they move through a divorce: they simply get into a business-like mentality, separate themselves from their emotions, and focus on taking care of whatever needs taking care of.

Then too, because men are often raised to be more competitive than women, there may be a greater desire to "win," even at the risk of irrevocably harming the relationship with their spouse.

Women, who tend to be more emotional and relational than men, generally have more concern for everyone's feelings during and after the divorce. They have a harder time separating their emotions about the marriage ending and their family splitting up from the business of divorce. An example of this might be a woman who is more inclined to give up something that may rightfully be hers, in an attempt to preserve the relationship with her spouse.

Obviously, either gender is capable of caring about the welfare of the other spouse or of being quite cutthroat, but it can be helpful to be aware that gender differences may exist and that they may come into play during the divorce (just as they may have during the marriage).

AFFIRMATION

I recognize that my spouse may have a different perspective on divorce than I do, and I allow for these differences.

JOURNAL EXERCISE

■ *Refer to the two tables below to answer the questions that follow:*

Table 1. Common Attitudes	
Leaver	**Leavee**
Guilty	In shock
Ready to move on	In denial

Table 2. Gender Differences	
Male	**Female**
All business	More emotional
Okay with win-lose	Okay with lose-win

1. *Do you see yourself or your spouse in any of these descriptions? If so, which descriptions and why?*

2. *Do these descriptions help to explain a behavior your spouse has demonstrated that may have hurt or angered you?*

3. *Consider an unkind or disagreeable behavior that you may have demonstrated. Is there anything about that behavior you'd be willing to work on? Do you need support in changing it?*

4. *Are there other major differences you can identify in your dissolution process?*

5. *What other observations have you made on this topic?*

34

THE VULNERABILITY
OF INTIMACY

*The easiest kind of relationship is with ten thousand
people. The hardest is with one.*

~ Joan Baez

Close, intimate relationships show you where your strengths
are; they also highlight the areas where you need to do your
internal work. It's easier to have many superficial relationships
than it is to maintain one deep and meaningful relationship.

Your spouse was someone with whom you likely shared
both extremes of your complete human spectrum: your best
self and your worst self. For that reason, you are more vulnerable to this one person because you've shared more of
yourself.

Furthermore, the more committed you are to another
person, the more is required of you—for example, having to
think of the other person in addition to yourself; having to

respond to the other person's needs when they've been communicated; and having to change your old ways of relating. This is one of the aspects of marriage that distinguishes it from all other relationships: if you are like most people, you exchanged vows promising this level of care and commitment to each other.

Now that you are divorcing, you may feel intense emotions that no one else on the planet could evoke from you, except your spouse. This is so precisely because you have been vulnerable to your spouse in your marriage.

As you heal from this relationship ending, you will feel less and less vulnerable and, if you choose to, you will be able to form a new relationship with your spouse from a place of renewed strength.

AFFIRMATION

I move through my divorce process feeling less vulnerable the more I heal.

JOURNAL EXERCISE

- *Write down three to five strengths you learned about yourself in your relationship with your spouse.*

- *Write down three to five weaknesses you learned about yourself in your relationship with your spouse.*

- *Write down three to five ways that you and your spouse worked well together.*

- *Write down three to five ways that you and your spouse provoked each other negatively.*

- *What, if anything, can you do to change this negative dynamic now that you are splitting up?*

35

FEAR AND AMBIVALENCE

How often my fear and ambivalence are rooted in what somebody else may think.

~ Jan Denise

Second-guessing a divorce is to be expected. Fearing that you or your spouse made the wrong decision, thinking about all that could go wrong with the divorce process and life afterward, and wondering about the right next steps are common mental and emotional responses during such a major life transition.

You are likely to feel some confusion and apprehension as you navigate the dissolution process, particularly if you've never been through a divorce before. Feeling unsure is not necessarily an indication that you are on the wrong track by divorcing, but it can certainly be unsettling if you don't know that feeling confused and apprehensive is a normal part of the process.

There may be ambivalence about the whole issue of the divorce itself, or you may feel indecisive about the particulars along the way, such as keeping or selling the house, who should stay in the house if it is not sold, how much time the kids should spend with each parent, which divorce professionals you should hire, and who should maintain certain expenses.

During this transition period, the crossroads that appear requiring you to make a choice may seem innumerable. Your feelings of insecurity about whether or not you are taking the right course of action are likely to be present much of the time. Short of having a crystal ball, you can't know for sure which choice to make, so it's important that you:

1. think things through as much as possible;

2. ask for the support and guidance you need;

3. allow for the fact that you may make mistakes along the way, and be kind to yourself if you do make mistakes.

As long as you take these three steps when making each decision put before you, you will be more likely to make the right decisions. You might not always have the luxury of enough time or of getting more information before making a decision, so it is all the more important that you not be too hard on yourself if you do err.

When making decisions related to their divorces, I often suggest to people that they write down: (1) their options before arriving at a decision, (2) the decision they made, and (3) the reasons why they made that decision. That way, they can look back and remember why they chose as they did or review the thinking that was behind their choice. This kind of record can go a long way toward being gentle with yourself later on.

AFFIRMATION

I accept my feelings of ambivalence with each choice presented to me, and I move through the process even so.

JOURNAL EXERCISE

- *As suggested above, make a list of the decisions you are being asked to make today as a result of your divorce. If you know what choice you will make, write it down as well as the explanation of why you are choosing that option. If you don't know what choice to make, you may want to create a list of pros and cons or a list of questions that you will bring to members of your support network to get their opinions.*

36

THE ART OF BEING ASSERTIVE

*Parents who are afraid to put their foot down usually
have children who step on their toes.*

~ Chinese proverb

As with any negotiation or business deal, each party in a marital dissolution can choose one of three ways of trying to reach a settlement and coexisting: passive, aggressive, or assertive.

To be passive is to allow whatever happens to happen. In a divorce situation, it is to allow your spouse to have whatever he or she wants in the settlement. Sometimes people do this out of guilt because they very much want to leave the marriage or they've done something wrong, or they may just be feeling impatient because they don't want to deal with the discomfort of, for example, dividing assets. Then there are cases when one spouse is dealing with an abusive partner and it's just easier to give in, and in some cases, it's safer.

Obviously, to be aggressive is the opposite of being passive. With aggressive situations, one or both parties to the divorce want everything they feel they have coming to them and perhaps more. For example, they may want full custody of the children, as much spousal support as possible, and as many of the assets as they can get.

Acting aggressively can also mean being obstructive— for example, not picking up the kids on a day when it's your responsibility (or picking them up when it's your spouse's turn), thus making life more difficult for your spouse. It can also mean flaunting your new relationship to your spouse or being purposely hurtful in some way.

These extreme ways of being aggressive during the divorce process almost always wreak tremendous damage on one or both spouses, as well as on the children involved. Most often people behave in these ways because they don't know any other way to be or because they are afraid to act differently.

They may be afraid they won't get what they want or need. This is one reason it's easier to hire an attorney to negotiate the settlement.

The middle ground between being passive or aggressive is to be assertive. This means standing up for what you believe but not at the other person's expense; stating what you need and working toward getting it; and making reasonable compromises if your spouse needs or wants something that is at cross-purposes with what you need or want.

Being assertive comes from being confident in yourself, while both passive and aggressive stances demonstrate a lack of self-confidence. People respect those who are assertive and don't respect those who are either passive or aggressive.

AFFIRMATION

I act with assertion today.

JOURNAL EXERCISE

- *What does being assertive mean to you?*

- *What are some of the ways you can be assertive in your divorce?*

- *Do you feel you have been passive or aggressive through your divorce process (or even during your marriage)? If so, how? Is this something you can change or get support with (that is, through your attorney)?*

EXERCISE

There are numerous books, classes, and resources on learning how to be assertive. If you feel you need assertiveness training, you can search the Internet, local libraries, local community college courses, adult education courses, or mental health facilities for information and resources.

37

PRIORITIES

You can tell how important something is today by mea-
suring its potential future impact on your life.

~ Brian Tracy

Much like an earthquake, the divorce process can make you feel as though your world has been turned upside down. Having been shaken to your core, you may feel tired, confused, and weakened. It may be difficult to know where or how to start to get through the dissolution and get your life back on track. Finding order in the mountain of tasks can seem impossible.

Much the way triage is used by doctors who deal with the wounded in wartime, taking care of the most pressing and basic matters first is critical: Are you safe from harm? Do you have a place to live? Do you have enough money to pay for your food, your shelter, and the daily needs of your children and yourself? What is your plan for the immediate future (that is, the next fifteen to thirty days)?

Although not everyone has to be concerned with this level of survival functioning, everyone does need to make sure these components are securely in place before moving on to the next tier of tasks. At this point, good resources are most helpful.

The second level of priorities may be in getting through the particulars of the divorce process—that is, filing the paperwork, hiring an attorney, and understanding your finances, both your assets and debts. Taking care of these tasks will help you move through the legal process and will shed some light on what you can expect life to look like postdivorce. At this point, good information is most helpful.

The third level of priorities may be in rebuilding your life. Important life choices must be made, such as where to live, which career or job to pursue, what school the kids will attend, how much custodial time each parent will have, how to relate to your children as a single parent and to the world as a single person, and what to do with free time (if you have any). Although this can be an exciting stage in the divorce process, it can also be very challenging. At this point, good support will be most helpful.

Within each tier of priorities, you will need to decide when each particular task before you should be addressed. Remember that you don't have to take care of everything at once. You can make a list of your priorities and begin with the most important one first.

If you're unclear on how to determine what action should receive the highest priority, make a list and determine which task will have the greatest impact on your life today and tomorrow. Such a list can bring great clarity and make your choices more obvious.

Divorce often feels daunting, and your emotions can get in the way of your better judgment. If you're still not sure where to start, ask for help from friends or professionals. All sorts of things will become clearer as you proceed.

AFFIRMATION

I will find order today. I will select one task as the most important to be done today and I will begin to create order in this chaos.

JOURNAL EXERCISE

- *Write out a tentative plan addressing one or all of the three tiers of priorities outlined above. First, list your immediate survival and safety needs; then list the tasks you must do to get through your divorce; and finally, list what you will need to begin your postdivorce life. Even if you don't know the answers yet, this exercise can help by showing you the areas you do need to focus on..*

- *Next, list what divorce resources, information, and support you currently have in place. If you need more, how will you go about finding them?*

38

GETTING QUIET

The quieter you become, the more you can hear.

~ Baba Ram Dass

During such tumultuous times as a marital dissolution, it can be extremely challenging to stay calm. There are so many unknowns, so many intense emotions, and so many details to tend to. As a result, the more stressed and overwhelmed you feel, the less quiet you are likely to be. Staying calm may feel counterintuitive.

Ironically, the thing you may be least inclined to do is the very best thing you can do for yourself. To demonstrate this point, I often use the analogy of the Chinese finger trap. When you place your index fingers in each end of a small, woven bamboo cylinder, they immediately become trapped. The more you pull, the more tightly the cylinder wraps around your fingers.

The key to getting free is to gently push the ends toward the middle. This action enlarges the openings and frees the fingers.

When getting divorced, most people are inclined to become anxious, more emotional, and more "busy-brained." Although this is understandable, the more time you can take to be quiet and grounded, the better you will be able to function. You will hear more clearly, see more clearly, listen better, and feel more connected to yourself.

Emotions–especially intense emotions—can distort all of your perceptions. If you have no way to keep these emotions in check, you will be at their mercy.

AFFIRMATION

I will give myself the gift of quiet solitude so that I can hear, see, listen, and feel better.

MEDITATION

In times when you find yourself becoming very emotional, take a five-minute time-out to ground yourself. Sit comfortably, take several deep breaths, relax your shoulders, and settle your mind.

Then, calmly recite some affirmations to yourself, as they can help a great deal in making you feel better in the moment.

Here are some ideas for affirmations:

- This will all work out.

- I am enough, I have enough, there is enough.

- This is temporary.

- I can ask for help when I need it.

- I am strong, centered, and grounded.

- Many people love me.

- The universe supports my success and recovery.

39

PERCEPTION

It's not what you look at that matters, it's what you see.

~ Henry David Thoreau

We all go through tough times; we've all felt the sting of rejection and disappointment when things don't go our way, we've all "failed" at something. However, what matters is not what happens to us in life but what we tell ourselves about what happens. The events in and of themselves are not the problem. The problem comes when reacting to these events, you tell yourself that you are unworthy, unlovable, and unsuccessful.

It's appropriate to feel bad, sad, or even mad in reaction to a "negative" life event such as your spouse leaving you or your marriage ending, but the degree to which you spiral downward can show you where you need to do some inner work and how much of it there is to do.

As an example of such inner work, suppose you have an old belief that deep down you are an unlovable person. Your inner work might include exploring when and how this belief originated and replacing it with a new belief, such as "I am lovable."

For one person, a rejection may be devastating because it triggers an unhealed wound from a past rejection. But for another person, a rejection may be viewed simply as the rejecter's loss.

Present-day happenings can help to heal wounds from the past when you pay attention to what's going on inside of yourself. Pay attention to the negative chatter taking place in your mind so that you can heal the wounds that need healing.

AFFIRMATION

I pay attention to my reactions to events so that I know what, where, and how much work I need to do on myself to heal.

JOURNAL EXERCISE

- *Write about any of the intense negative emotions that have come up during your divorce process. Also write about any other time in your life when you felt similar feelings—that is, when you felt you had failed, were rejected, or were unworthy.*

- *What were the circumstances? What are the similarities between then and now?*

- *What within you needs to be healed? How can you heal it?*

40

RESISTANCE TO CHANGE

Weep not that the world changes—did it keep a stable, changeless state, it were cause indeed to weep.

~William Cullen Bryant

One of the characteristics of being human is that we are creatures of habit. As such, most of us resist change, even if it is of our own making and even when it's in our best interest. This occurs in small habits as well as large ones. Change requires us to move away from our old habits both in thought and action and to create new ways of relating to ourselves and the world around us.

Giving up that which you've known, lived with, and identified yourself by, perhaps for a long time, can be very challenging. For most people, the transition between being married and being divorced is not an easy time because so many areas of your life are greatly affected. And it's not just a matter of living in a different home than your spouse.

If you have children, you may have to share custody and learn how to coparent from separate households. Even if you don't have children, you will have to adjust to the loss of your spouse. Some people getting divorces have to change residences. Some must find new jobs or get back into the workforce. Extended family and friend relationships must be redefined. Finances and budgets change. This list could go on and on.

The older you are, the more set in your ways you are likely to be. Having the willingness to be a beginner will serve you well. This entails doing new things, even when these things are not comfortable; asking for help, even when you think you should be able to handle something or that you should know the answer; trusting others to guide you, even when you have no idea of where you are headed.

AFFIRMATION

I move through the changes in my life with willingness and grace.

JOURNAL EXERCISE

- *Write about the changes you have gone through to date as a result of your marital dissolution. Which of these changes have been easy for you and which have been the most challenging? Why were some changes easy and others hard? What have you done to make* the transitions easier for yourself (emotionally, mentally, and physically)?

■ What changes are you currently resisting making? Why? If they are inevitable changes, what can you do to have a better experience? What kind of resources do you need to help you as you make those changes?

41

TRUE FRIENDS

The only service a friend can really render is to keep up your courage by holding up to you a mirror in which you can see a noble image of yourself.

~ George Bernard Shaw

You really find out who your friends are when you're going through the highest and lowest points in your life. Those who are jealous of your successes or judgmental of you when things don't go as planned are not acting as true friends should.

Because divorce inherently carries so many charged emotions for everyone, this event more than most others reveals who are your true friends and who are not. This is so for several reasons: some people still carry pain associated with their own divorces; some fear that divorce is contagious and if it's happening to you, then it could happen to them; others don't know how to relate to you as a single person, so they stop calling, inviting you to visit, and being there for you.

If someone you thought of as a good friend can't support you during your marital dissolution, you may need to put the relationship with your friend on hold until after your divorce has been finalized. You may even realize that some "friends" aren't worthy of the name, and you may want to let them go altogether.

At an already loss-filled time, it can be excruciating to lose a friend on top of all the other losses you are experiencing. However, it's essential at this time to have good, supportive people in your life—people who raise your spirits, who are there when you need to vent, who believe in you and want you to see you intact on the other side of your divorce, emotionally, mentally, physically, and spiritually.

Be open and inviting to those who clearly are there for you in the way you need them to be. Choose to spend time only with those who support you right now. Who you surround yourself with can make a huge difference in how you feel about yourself and how well you do during and after your divorce.

AFFIRMATION

I choose only supportive people to be in my life today.

JOURNAL EXERCISE

- *Make a list of three to five people you consider to be your best friends. Next to each person's name, write down the ways they have been there for you, and the ways they may have let you down at this turning point in your life.*

- *What did you learn? Did anything you wrote surprise you at all? If so, what and why? What, if any, actions do you need to take to improve the quality of the friendships you have?*

42

BEING STRETCHED

I know God will not give me anything I can't handle.
I just wish that He didn't trust me so much.

~ Mother Teresa

Most losses stretch us beyond what we think we can handle, yet not only can we survive, we can ulitmately thrive. Although it may be very painful, when we are pulled out of our comfort zone and made to deal with things we don't think we can handle or shouldn't have to, we become a little more deeply rooted within ourselves.

Pain is said to be the touchstone for growth. Left to our own devices, most of us stay inside our comfort zone, or if we do choose to stretch, it is to a manageable level. It is highly unlikely that we would ever stretch to levels of great pain of our own volition.

It is only when something drastic comes along to push us that we are forced to grow so much. Divorce often propels people to stretch themselves to the extreme emotionally, mentally, socially, and financially.

But what if you knew that the Universe was not giving you more than you can handle? What if you knew that you truly could get through this time and face what there is in front of you to face? Would that help to make this time more bearable?

It can be quite helpful to talk to others with similar stories who have gotten through the divorce process intact. Just knowing that they survived can give you hope that you will survive too. Hearing that divorce is challenging—but doable— can be enough to help you trust that there is a strength or power within you that, until now, has gone untapped. It is a power that will get you through this transition.

Perhaps now is as good a time as any to start learning to trust that things do happen for a reason. There is a bigger picture than what you can see now, and you actually can stretch way beyond where you think you can.

AFFIRMATION

I can handle all that I am being asked to handle right now.

EXERCISE

Find at least two other people who have been through a divorce under similar circumstances (for example, they too were left by their spouse for a younger person, or they thought everything was fine until their spouse abruptly left), and interview them. Ask them how they got through their experience and what advice they would give to you to help you get through yours. Ask them if they would be available for calls from you, what books they would recommend, and what not to do (for example, what they did during their divorce that made things worse for them or their spouse).

JOURNAL EXERCISE

- *Write down what the people you found to interview for the above exercise told you, and refer to this writing whenever you begin to doubt that you can endure the pain.*

43

DARK DAYS

It's always darkest before the dawn.

~ Proverb

Most people in the thick of a divorce fear that these divorcing days—perhaps some of the darkest days of their lives—are indicative of how the rest of their lives will be. This is a common thought that anyone undergoing a challenging time has: fearing it will never end. However, the point at which change for the better occurs is often just when matters are at their worst.

It's important to be able to endure the rough times, but knowing they will end may help you to not give up. Time does pass more slowly when we are not living in a good space; nonetheless, time still passes. Eventually, you will reach a place from which you'll look back on this period. Then, you'll have a different perspective, and you'll see that, indeed, you have changed, grown, and healed.

While divorce makes daily life more challenging for many, it is not necessarily true that the quality of your life will stay diminished for the duration of your life. Although sometimes divorce makes getting ahead financially a bit more challenging, it can also be an event that inspires those going through it to go back to school, put in for a promotion, or change careers. Divorce can be the springboard for living a more expanded life.

The key that determines which type of experience you have is whether or not you get appropriate support. I have never seen anyone who has reached out for help and guidance not land on his or her feet after having received the help and guidance they asked for. Perhaps seeking assistance is indicative of a person who wants to have a better experience, but I think the improved outcome is the *result* of getting the support.

AFFIRMATION

I endure the tough times knowing they will eventually pass.

JOURNAL EXERCISE

- *Reflect on other periods in your life during which you had to endure challenges. Do you remember fearing that the challenge would never end? Write about what that was like for you.*

■ *Then write about how and why you believe the situation improved. Certainly time passing is always a factor, but think of other factors too, such as a best friend whose support was lifesaving, the right opportunity for positive change presenting itself due to a lucky break, or hard work on your part.*

■ *Can any of the things that helped you before be helpful to you now? If so, what? What do you need to do to make that happen?*

44

SECURITY

There is no security on this earth, there is only opportunity.

~ General Douglas MacArthur

Actual security doesn't exist. In any given day, all that any of us has is a sense of security. We surround ourselves with all things familiar, and we take actions and think thoughts that make us feel more in control of our environment. We build structures that we think will never tumble, we set up certain jobs with tenure, and we have the institution of marriage that is supposed to last forever. But life has a way of keeping us humble, and we see that some of the things we believed would be forever are not always forever.

Thinking we have security isn't a design flaw in our species. In fact, it's quite the opposite. If none of us felt safe and secure, we wouldn't be able to take risks or venture into unknown territory. Having a sense of security helps us to grow and change.

When life throws us a curve ball, it is our sense of security that is broken, not our actual security (since that doesn't exist).

It's normal to feel let down (or even betrayed) when something we thought we could or should count on doesn't last or proves untrustworthy. But even with the best of intentions, no one can promise anything forever; everything "permanent" can be changed, and any security we have is merely a sense of security. We can certainly take actions to diminish the chances that our security will be threatened, but nothing we do is foolproof.

Understanding this can change your perspective on what you are experiencing. It can also facilitate your acceptance of your divorce situation, which, in turn, will facilitate your movement through the grief process.

It's not wrong to want to feel secure, but it's unrealistic to believe that you are immune from events that will shake your foundation. Absolute security doesn't exist for anyone, anywhere. With this in mind, enjoy the times when you do feel secure, knowing that it is a comfortable and necessary illusion.

AFFIRMATION

I enjoy my sense of security, knowing that real security is an illusion.

JOURNAL EXERCISE

■ *Write down all the experiences you have had in your life that you thought were secure but were not. How did you regain your feeling of security?*

■ *How will your view on life change knowing that security is nothing more than an illusion? Will you make different choices? Will you appreciate what you have more?*

45

PLANTING SEEDS

It helps beyond words to plant bulbs in the dark of winter.

~ Anne Lamott

Taking actions today to create a better life for yourself tomorrow is a powerful act. It brings hope and a sense of empowerment that can be indescribably important during such dark times as a marital dissolution.

It may help you to realize that every thought you have today, every action you take today, and every intention you set today is moving you in a particular direction. Good questions to ask yourself are: "Is this the direction I want to be headed in?" "Are these the seeds I want to be sowing today for the life I want to create tomorrow?" If the answers are negative, then you may want to rethink what you are setting in motion.

Certain realities you have to attend to in the process of divorcing may make you feel as though you are stuck in the mud, such as having to wade through the legal paperwork and keep track of court dates. You must also grieve the loss of your relationship, your family, and your dream. These aspects of divorce take time; there are no shortcuts around them.

That said, as you proceed with your divorce, it's okay to start thinking about what you would like your future to look like. It's also fine to begin creating new habits and fostering new friendships. By taking actions such as these, you can make the challenging "stuck" times more bearable. You will have one eye on the things immediately before you and one on the direction in which you are headed.

AFFIRMATION

In the midst of my divorce, I will plant the seeds of new thoughts, feelings, and habits in preparation for my new life.

JOURNAL EXERCISE

- *Write out the tasks you must do regarding your divorce in the weeks and months ahead of you so that you don't lose sight of them. Once you have written these down, take a few minutes to write down ten ways in which you would like your new life to be different (for example, I'll be able to stay out as late as I want, I will manage my money better, I will do more fun things with my kids).*

■ *If you want to bring new people into your life, spend a minute to write down some of the qualities these new people should possess (for example, mature, trustworthy, fun, lighthearted).*

MEDITATION

If you are moved to do so, spend some time envisioning how your new life will feel. Close your eyes and see yourself living your new life. Feel these new feelings, and perhaps write about your envisioning experience when you are done.

46

AN UNRESOLVED HEART

Be patient with all that is unresolved in your heart.

~ Rainer Maria Rilke

Ending a marriage or a long-term relationship leaves empty spaces in the hearts of those who are grieving. These empty spaces cannot be filled with just any new thing. Enough time needs to pass to fully heal the heart and soul. Waiting for this to happen is one of the hardest parts of getting to the other side of the divorce process.

There is a saying that "the only way out is through," and this definitely applies to anyone grieving. There are no short-cuts. And often, the more you try to control or stop yourself from feeling the sadness, pain, and hurt, the more you actually prolong these feelings because you're not allowing them to be. It is only by sitting with the discomfort and allowing it to be—that is, allowing yourself to really feel your pain—that the emotions eventually diminish and the healing can take place.

What you need to know and understand is that a state such as depression or intense sadness is a healthy and appropriate response to the end of your marriage. You may not feel this sadness right away, or as intensely as someone else who has been through a divorce, but your pain is your pain. Do what you can to acknowledge it and let it be what it is. Eventually it will pass and you will heal.

AFFIRMATION

I cannot force my heart to feel whole again. I will wait for resolution patiently.

MEDITATION

Find a quiet and comfortable place to lie down or, if you prefer, sit in a comfortable chair. If you like, wrap yourself in a blanket, then curl up into a ball, and just stay with your broken heart. Feel the pain of the hurt, sadness, and perhaps anger that your marriage did not last. The broken dreams, broken hearts, and broken promises of life are painfully unfair; allow yourself to feel all of the emotions you have about them.

47

BUILDING COMMUNITY

But the most daring thing is to create stable communities
in which the terrible disease of loneliness can be cured.

~ Kurt Vonnegut, Jr.

Losing friendships and your sense of belonging can be a very real and unfortunate side effect of divorce. Social circles change once you go from being part of a married couple to being a single person. This is so for a variety of reasons, such as group alliances, social awkwardness, emotional insecurities, and more.

Know that those who are your true friends will continue to be your true friends and those who are not will fade away in time. Certainly, it's important to grieve these losses, but losing these people from your life doesn't need to be the end of your sense of community.

Initially, you may feel as though there are no single people in your world with whom you can relate and share interests, but most likely, that's not the case. There are many wonderful single people, but since you haven't been hanging out in the same social circles, you haven't met them yet.

Joining a group for divorcing people can be an excellent way of not only meeting single people, but meeting divorcing people. Often, talking to others in similar life situations can be more helpful than sharing with those who haven't been through that experience.

Calling someone who is in the same boat tends to be easier not only because she understands your pain and is less likely to grow tired of your calls (as you may fear others do), but because you can also be there for her if she needs to bend your ear. It's a mutual exchange rather than one-sided, as it might be with a sister or best friend who is not going through a divorce.

If you can't find a divorce support group through a local church or therapy center, you may want to try starting your own. Although a support group may not be right for everyone, there are other things you can do with members of your divorcing community, like going to the movies, creating a book club, or hosting a Saturday night dinner club.

Creating a new community will be key in your recovery from divorce. You will gain strength and resources from that community that would take you much longer to manifest and organize on your own. The community doesn't have to be composed only of divorcing people, but it can make a big difference to have at least one person in your circle who understands what you are going through so that you won't feel so isolated.

Being single can make you feel vulnerable in and of itself. Trying to join or create a new community for yourself may magnify the sense of being exposed to the world, but when you succeed, you will be so glad you reached out.

AFFIRMATION

I am creating a new community of wonderful single people.

EXERCISE

Check your local resources (search the Internet, bulletin boards, and newspapers) to see what exists in the way of a divorce recovery group or community. If there is something already organized near you, commit to looking into whether this would be right for you.

If you don't feel it's a good fit, would you be willing to start your own group, such as a movie or book club? Would you be willing to attend a new class in order to meet people? What else can you do to create a new community?

48

FEELING HATRED

The opposite of love is not hate. It is indifference.

~ Mal Pancoast

When any relationship ends, it's not uncommon for one or both partners to feel intense hatred for the other at some point. There are several reasons this can occur. Some people feel intense dislike for their spouse even before their marriage ends. They may feel this when they believe their trust has been betrayed. Or they may feel it as a response to a great deal of mental or emotional damage experienced during their marital relationship, which may continue happening until they decide to divorce. Some people need to feel this hatred in order to justify leaving the relationship. Their intense anger is used to separate (or even repel) them from their spouse.

The second instance of hatred arises in response to feeling rejected by the other spouse. Perhaps one spouse has expressed dissatisfaction with the marriage that wasn't anticipated, or one spouse behaved badly, such as having had an affair or refusing to participate in family functions. When we are hurt, one natural reaction is to become angry. Hate stems from intense anger.

During divorce proceedings, there are many opportunities to feel hatred toward your spouse. It can crop up when your spouse handles something in a sly or underhanded way, asks for too much, or requests something to which he may be legally entitled, but which you think he should not ask for. The fact that this person whom you married and with whom you may have had children can be so insensitive to your needs can create very strong negative feelings.

Finally, there may be hate even after the relationship is legally dissolved and the divorce is finalized. This hate can come about as a result of feeling that your spouse "ruined" your life or was untrustworthy, or because you saw her true colors come out during the legal proceedings.

Having this intense level of emotion present throughout a divorce is not abnormal. It's actually indicative of how attached you were to your spouse. Although we sometimes use anger to push others away, in another sense we stay intensely connected to whomever we are furious with. They live rent-free in our minds, where we imagine what we'd like to say or do to them. Or we use up a lot of our energy just thinking about them.

You don't despise your spouse because you don't care for him or her anymore. When you despise someone to whom you've been close, you still have an emotional connection to that person. Indifference is the true opposite of love, because it means there is no longer an emotional connection between you and your spouse.

Only when you reach the place called indifference will you know that you are on the other side of the healing process. When you are indifferent to your ex-spouse, you will know that you've worked through the pain that you experienced in your marriage. You can't will yourself to be indifferent, but you can certainly think of indifference as a goal you want to reach.

AFFIRMATION

I am closer every day to the freedom that indifference brings.

JOURNAL EXERCISE

■ *Make a list of all the reasons why you feel or have felt hatred toward your spouse. If you have any insights as to how you can work to heal from this intense emotion, then write about that. Keep this list and check it each month or so to see how connected you still are to that emotion. If you continue to feel an emotional charge, you still have some healing to do. If you don't, and you feel nothing, then you will know that you have reached indifference.*

49

PERSPECTIVE

You can't see the forest for the trees.

~ Traditional proverb

When you are in the midst of your marital troubles or the divorce process, you may not be able to imagine your life without the struggle and strife you've experienced. You're too immersed in your day-to-day problems to see that there is a solution.

Given that you may have endured (and continue to endure) hard times with your spouse, you may have come to believe that this is your lot in life. But it is not. Although you may have to deal with the particulars of your situation in the moment, it's important for you to realize that there is a big picture beyond the minutia you are living with right now.

The reason this is important is that it can give you perspective. When people have perspective, they often make different decisions than when they lack it. For example, if you believe that you will be in a draining power struggle with your spouse for the next ten years because the two of you fought for the past ten years, you will think, feel, and act differently than if you believe that the battling will be over soon.

You may feel hopeless, oppressed, and depressed thinking about your glum future. You may stop trying and stop caring about things. When you feel strongly, however, that there can be another outcome for all of your challenges, it's likely that you will begin to feel some hope and, perhaps, some empowerment. You will feel that your actions today do make a difference for outcomes tomorrow, and you may even see the changes happening all around you.

If you have lost perspective on your situation, it may be time to reach out to your friends and extended family and ask them to help you gain perspective. Ask them these questions: What do they think of your relationship? What would they recommend to improve your situation? What insights and wisdom can they impart to you?

You may want to talk to someone you know who has finished with his or her divorce process (ideally, someone with circumstances similar to yours), hear about how that person got through it, and learn about how that person is doing now. The more information you have, the more perspective you are likely to have and the better the decisions you make will be.

A word of caution: be sure that the people you seek counsel from are supportive and nonjudgmental. Otherwise, you may end up feeling worse about your situation and yourself.

AFFIRMATION

With each passing day, I get a clearer and clearer perspective on my life.

JOURNAL EXERCISE

- *Write about the perspective you currently have on your relationship with your spouse. If you feel hopeless, oppressed, or depressed, why do you feel this way? What other emotions are you experiencing?*

- *Next, write about how you would like your life to be. Where will you be living? What will you be doing (working, volunteering, learning new skills)? What kinds of people will you associate with?*

- *What else can you do to gain perspective and see the bigger picture for your life?*

- *Whom can you talk to?*

- *What actions can you take today to move you closer to your vision?*

50

YOU ARE LOVED

In a world filled with hate, we must dare to hope. In a world filled with anger, we must still dare to comfort. In a world filled with despair, we must still dare to dream. And in a world filled with distrust, we must still dare to believe.

~ Michael Jackson

One of the greatest fears divorcing people may have is how society will view them once their divorce has been finalized. They fear they will be seen as failures, as two- or three-time losers, as rejects, lustful cheats, or somehow deeply flawed.

But the fact is that thousands of people divorce every day all over the world. You are not alone. Yet despite the large numbers of divorces, some social stigma still lingers.

How another person reacts to your divorce says more about that person than it does about you. If that person shows disdain or even disgust, this indicates their ignorance of what your divorce situation is all about.

In general, when we feel better about ourselves, we aren't as influenced by the opinions of others. If someone feels disgust or disdain for your divorced status, but you are at peace with it, it won't bother you so much.

If you are affected by the opinions of those around you, it is an indication that you are being too hard on yourself and that you need healing. In order to heal, you must become more conscious of the negative self-talk you may be experiencing. How do *you* feel about the fact that you are divorcing? What do *you* think it means to be divorced? What judgment do *you* make about yourself or your spouse for being in this place? What are *you* afraid of? When have *you* ever felt this way before? What in *you* needs healing?

Regardless of the circumstances of your divorce, you can use this opportunity to heal any old scars you may have about being unloved or unlovable. These painful emotions may be easier for you to access now. You are quite vulnerable to feeling unworthy because you are experiencing a major loss, not because you are a failure or because you did something wrong.

Be gentle, get support if you need it, but go beneath the surface layer of chatter to find out what old wound may be presenting itself to be healed. Know that you are completely lovable, especially now while you are broken open.

AFFIRMATION

I am loved and I am lovable.

JOURNAL EXERCISE

- *Referring to the questions below, write in your journal about your experience. There may be more than one issue that comes to mind, so write about it all or whatever you feel comfortable addressing.*

- *If nothing comes to mind, then it could be that you are not emotionally strong enough to go to this level of introspection. Simply revisit this chapter at a later point in your divorce proceedings and try again. Don't push for results.*

1. *How do you feel about the fact that you are divorcing?*

2. *What do you think it means to be divorced?*

3. *What judgment do you hold toward yourself or your spouse for being in this place?*

4. *What are you afraid of?*

5. *When have you felt this way before?*

6. *What within you needs healing?*

- *As you answer these questions, feel free to write about anything else that comes up for you.*

51

THE NEW NORMAL

The secret of your future is hidden in your daily routine.

~ Mike Murdock

Life during the process of divorce and sometimes for a period postdivorce can be rocky. Marital dissolution is one of the greatest transitions you may ever face, so it's important to understand that it's typical for it to take a while to find your "new normal," and to arrive at the calm that follows the storm.

Given the fact that you are adjusting to life as a single person and perhaps adjusting as a single parent as well, it makes sense that finding balance again will not be simple. There are many new social norms and challenges to deal with as a newly single person. There may be ongoing adjustments and lifestyle changes that will have to be made for quite a while following divorce.

We all like to feel safe in our environment. A new normal is what you are seeking, but it is not something that can be forced. Rather, it's a series of new routines that are settled into by repeating new behaviors over time.

It's important to be aware that everything you do today is creating new habits and laying the foundation for your new routines later on. Ask yourself if you are thinking and acting in a way that will enhance happiness in your new life or will impede it. This goes for habits of thought as well as physical habits.

Bringing your awareness to your thoughts and actions means that you have the power to change them if they are not the foundation you would like to have for going forward. One of the reasons divorce is so challenging is that it takes people so far out of their comfort zone and requires them to make changes to their daily life.

Major life events such as this take away your old sense of normalcy, but once things begin to calm down, you will develop a new normal. What will you set in motion today with your thoughts and actions?

AFFIRMATION

I am creating my new life today with every thought I have and every action I take.

JOURNAL EXERCISE

- *At the end of the day, write down ten or more thoughts you had during the day. These can be anything from an observation you made to a reaction you had to what another person said or did. What patterns do you notice? Are any of these thoughts that you have never had before, or do you have such thoughts often?*

- *If you are inclined to change these thoughts, what would you want to think instead? Write down these new thoughts on an index card and place it in a conspicuous place. Read these new thoughts aloud to yourself as many times a day as you can remember to do it. This activity can retrain your brain to think these new thoughts more automatically.*

- *Repeat this exercise writing down ten or more actions you took today. Write about your reaction to your awareness about your behavior. Then write about any patterns you notice. Finally, what are you willing to commit to doing in order to change the behaviors you would like to change?*

52

SOLUTIONS AND PROBLEMS

The chief cause of problems is solutions.

~ Eric Sevareid

For every solution you come up with to deal with a challenge, other problems cannot help but arise. This holds true for any area in which you are facing challenges, be it your home, work, family, or social life. The reason for this is that everything in life has its own set of problems.

Let's look at how this dynamic can play out in a marriage and divorce situation.

A single woman enjoys her independence but feels lonely. She feels that something is missing in her life. So she dates to avoid feeling lonely. But dating makes her feel insecure.

She finally meets someone she can settle down with. As great as he is, relationships are complicated and require compromise. To build a life with him, she must leave her sweet home and move in with him. But she misses her sweet home and she misses her independence.

As they progress in their life together, they have children. They both had dreamt about creating a family. They love their children and family but now they fight more often. Creating a family filled a void each had felt, but now it is wreaking havoc on their relationship.

They seek support in the way of therapy and child care, but these cost a lot of money and put a financial strain on them. They work better as coparents but now they are having a hard time making ends meet.

She changes jobs to bring in more money. Now they have enough money to pay for the extras but she is quite stressed from her new job. The marital relationship endures even more problems.

She is unhappy in her marriage and feels she would be better off alone. They divorce and matters do improve between them, but now the stress of sharing child custody and living on a tight budget creates yet a new challenge. She is happy that the marital quarreling has ended but she finds she is still tense and anxious trying to get through each day as a single mom.

Although this is a very simplified version of what some-one's life and problems might look like, the point of this example is to show that each solution that this woman found for a specific problem had trade-offs. There was no solution that did not bring a different set of problems.

So the question is not "How do I avoid problems?" The question is always "Which choice brings better problems with it?" Or "Which avenue has challenges that I can live with?" Between A and B, which option has more good than bad?

AFFIRMATION

I accept that there is no solution without a new set of problems. Therefore, I choose wisely today, accepting the bad with the good.

JOURNAL EXERCISE

- *Write about the choices you've made in your life that have been solutions to problems. List the problems you solved and then the new problems that arose as a result of your solutions.*

- *Although you can't turn back the clock, you can use what you've learned here to know that no matter what road you are on in life, there will be challenges ahead that must be accepted and dealt with.*

53

LETTING GO OF YOUR STORY IN ORDER TO HEAL

Too often the pain from our past and our fears of the future keep us stuck and unable to see our lives as a whole.

~ Debbie Ford

Heather was a woman who was completely shocked by her husband's abrupt announcement one day that he was unhappy and that he was leaving her immediately. She had thought that everything in the marriage was going along fine. (She later found out that he had met someone else and was living with her.)

After he left, she didn't hear from him for three months. It was as if he had suddenly died and left her alone to care for their two young children. He didn't call her and he didn't contact their children. She had to pick up the pieces and try to make life go on as usual while also dealing with her grief and sense of devastation.

When the kids asked where their father was or when he'd be back, she had to tell them she didn't know. When they cried because they missed their dad, she had to comfort them. It was not easy. Understandably, she felt a swirling of intense emotions going on within herself every day.

Then one day, three months after he'd left, her husband came back and apologized to her. He said he didn't know what had gotten into him and that he now realized his actions had been wrong. By this time, however, the damage had been done and there was no longer any trust or connection between them. They agreed to divorce.

Heather was so hurt that she was sure she would never, ever recover from the breakup of her marriage. She was also sure that her children would be scarred for life. Heather very much identified herself as the victim of her husband's utter disregard for her and their kids. She felt that his actions were so cruel that no amount of apologizing or the passing of time could heal the wounds. She feared she would be the one person on the planet who would never recover from her divorce.

I often tell people that they will know they have let go when they no longer identify themselves by their divorce. Heather could not imagine ever being in this place.

Heather went through the divorce proceedings, moved to a new home, got the kids situated in a new life, and was even on speaking terms with her ex, but she truly believed that she would never trust anyone again.

It took her a long time to heal, and a great deal of therapy, self-help, and support, but eventually, Heather did indeed move to the other side of her pain. She was able to stop identifying herself by her husband's abandonment and started seeing herself as the powerful woman she had become as a result of her challenges. She even began seeing her husband's actions as a positive turn of events.

To the same degree that Heather had been knocked down, she began to feel good about herself and her life. As she got better, her kids also got stronger, and there was healing for them, too.

It did take a great deal of work and quite a long time, but because Heather hung in there, she did eventually reach the other side and can now testify to the fact that there really was another side to her ordeal—even for her.

AFFIRMATION

I will recover from my divorce.

JOURNAL EXERCISE

- *Whether or not you've been hurt in a way similar to the way that Heather was, you have a "story." Write down your story in your journal. Revisit it every month to see if and how it has changed. You may be surprised by what you find.*

54

TRY SOMETHING NEW

If you keep doing what you've always done, you'll keep getting what you've always got.

~ W. L. Bateman

Doing the same thing over and over but expecting to see a different result is a great way to set yourself up to feel bad. Some people even define that behavior as insane. To continue repeating behaviors and thoughts that do not work erodes our self-esteem. Yet we all do this to some degree.

When we feel bad about ourselves, we blame ourselves for those aspects of our lives that are not working. We tell ourselves, "If I just try harder or do more, it will work." We think we are flawed, and so we think our actions are insufficient. However, when we feel good about ourselves, we know we are not flawed. We may give someone another chance, but we don't keep on behaving in the same old way. We move on, we ask questions, and we make changes.

Ironically, more often than not, trying a new behavior will reward you with the results you are seeking. An example of these dynamics can be found in the person who always says yes when she means no. The reason she says yes is that she wants people to like her, but the fact that she says yes and has no apparent boundaries causes others to disrespect her and take advantage of her. Rather than being more liked for saying yes, she is less liked. If she said no occasionally and put her own needs first, others would feel more respect for her and might like her better.

If you are someone who has a history of repeating behaviors that don't serve you, try something different. If you've never asked for what you need, try it. If you've never said no when asked for something, say no!

AFFIRMATION

I will try a new behavior today in an attempt to get different results.

JOURNAL EXERCISE

- *Do you see areas of your life in which you repeat a behavior or a pattern that makes you feel bad or contributes to others treating you badly? If so, write about why you think this repetitive behavior got started. Why are you afraid to stop this behavior?*

EXERCISE

Consult a trusted friend or a therapist and talk about this behavior with that person. Talk about what you think you do and ask if they have seen you do this. Also ask them what they think you could do differently to get different results. Write down their responses and try out their suggestions in a safe environment, perhaps even with that trusted friend or therapist.

55

YOUR LIFE AFTER DIVORCE

Oh, my friend, it's not what they take away from you that counts. It's what you do with what you have left.

~ William Cowper

One of the toughest aspects of divorce is having to give up parts of the life you've worked so hard to put together. Most often, this means less money, fewer assets, less time with the kids, and less time for yourself. The contrast between pre-divorce, mid-divorce, and postdivorce lifestyles can be challenging to adjust to, particularly when the changes are still fresh. It can be tempting to stay focused on everything you've lost and to feel anger, resentment, betrayal, or hurt that your spouse has "taken" these things from you.

Almost no one walks away from a divorce saying that he or she enjoyed the experience. Also, most people feel that at least one major aspect of the division of assets or the child custody schedule was not fair. Although these feelings can be a normal part of the grief process, if the upset over your losses goes on for too long, it can prevent you from focusing on what you need to do in order to move on in your new life.

Because each divorce is so distinct in its details, no one can say exactly how long you should grieve your losses, but most people know when they have crossed the line of looking too long in the rear view mirror. There is an inner knowledge that their sights should be set on what's ahead.

Each time you have to do something, it reminds you of what you are missing or had to give up. There is no question but that life after divorce is harder in many ways. Yet asking for help and making the best of your situation are the key tools that will help you get through the entire process better.

Life will get easier in time if for no other reason than because you will have become accustomed to your new reality, and you will make the best of what you do have.

AFFIRMATION

I make the best of what I have today.

JOURNAL EXERCISE

- *As a way to validate your experience that life seems harder, write down some of the areas you now find more challenging. This exercise does not mean to imply that you should dwell on these difficulties; rather, it is meant to highlight where you now need more support.*

163

Write down one or two ways that you might be able to get more support in each of these more difficult areas.

■ *In order to balance your perspective on life after divorce, write down the ways in which your life has become easier as a result of your divorce. You may want to write these down on index cards and review them at the times when you are feeling low or overwhelmed during your divorce proceedings and afterward.*

56

FAITH

Faith does not rely on knowing anything with certainty. It requires only the courage to accept that whatever happens is for the highest good.

~ Dan Millman

"Everything happens for a reason," goes the old saying. If you believe this, it can certainly make you feel better. However, when life sends you events that most people would consider tragic, it's hard to imagine that there would be any reason—let alone a good reason—for the tragedy to have happened.

Although divorce is not usually seen as a tragic event, for most of those who experience it, the marital dissolution marks a major turning point in their lives—one that causes a level of pain and fallout similar to the effects of a natural disaster, such as an earthquake.

Divorce is rarely seen as a positive life event; however, in addition to its negative impacts, it also can have many positive effects on one or both spouses, their children, their extended families, and their friends. Sometimes these benefits are obvious when there is a great deal of animosity between spouses (especially in cases of physical or emotional abuse). Two people who do not bring out the best in each other will likely lead more peaceful emotional lives apart. If there are children, they are also likely to be emotionally healthier when they are not exposed to very high levels of tension, anger, and fighting.

At other times, however, the "highest good" reason to divorce may not be so apparent, and it may not become evident for a long time. For example, perhaps you've never lived alone and you need to learn that you can make a life for yourself. Perhaps some years after your divorce, you will meet someone much better suited to you than your ex-spouse was. Perhaps prior to getting divorced you were quite judgmental about divorced people, but now you've gained a deeper understanding and you've become more compassionate.

Keep an open mind concerning the possibility that there is an important reason for your divorce that may not be discernible to you today. One day that reason may become clear to you, and then you will understand the benefit you and perhaps others gained from your divorce. Keep an open mind that someday you will understand much more than you do now.

AFFIRMATION

I believe that my divorce is happening for the highest good of everyone involved.

JOURNAL EXERCISE

The process of looking for the positive elements will help you to shift your perspective in order to find those positive elements.

- *List five positive things that have come into your life as a result of your marital dissolution, no matter how trivial. (For example, you've learned how to ask for help, you are stronger than you thought you were, you feel calmer in your own skin, or now you can get rid of that unsightly red armchair.)*

- *Revisit this list every two months and add to it as you can.*

57

BECOMING MORE CONSCIOUS

There is no coming to consciousness without pain.

~ Carl Jung

Divorce has a way of bringing you face to face with yourself whether you like it or not. It is a growth experience unlike any other because of how much stigma is still attached to it and the sense of personal responsibility that is often associated with it. (For example, "I should have tried harder," "We married too young," "All he had to do was be honest.")

Certainly, there are people who don't use their divorce as an opportunity to learn about themselves (they may delve even further into distractions to keep from confronting themselves), but what they don't realize is that they cannot completely escape dealing with their "stuff." This is particularly true for the person who jumps right into a new relationship, or the person who becomes addicted to work or develops a dependence on alcohol or drugs. These may be temporary diversions, but ultimately there is no eluding whatever lessons you are meant to learn.

Furthermore, I believe that if you miss the lesson the first time around, the Universe has a way of turning up the volume, which translates into more drama, more pain, and more stuff to clean up, until you start paying attention and become conscious of what has previously been unconscious. Consciousness is defined as being awake or as having inner awareness.

This inner work consists of examining your part in the relationship dynamics, both the good and the bad; admitting when and where you were wrong; making amends; and perhaps going to therapy to try to uncover and change outdated beliefs and behavior patterns that may have set you up to engage in unhealthy relationships.

Most people don't do deep psychological work on themselves unless they are in pain or they experience the same unhealthy behavior over and over and over again. The reward for doing the inner work is that the part of you that was trying to get your attention no longer has to create painful events to get you to see what it is you need to learn.

An addict is an iconic example of someone who does not want to really see himself or herself (and this is true regardless of the type of addiction). Often, the addict uses the addictive substance as a way to not feel certain emotions or face particular memories, but because these emotions and memories don't go away, the addict must continue to use the substance to make "it" go away.

Because the "it" needs acknowledgment to heal, that old emotion or memory will try even harder to come to the surface to be healed. This frightens the addict even more, so she needs to use more of the substance to drown her pain. This cycle can go on for only so long before some kind of mental, emotional, or physical breakdown will occur. Then the addict is broken open and has no choice but to heal. At that point, there is no more running and hiding.

Some people have a higher threshold for pain than others, but eventually, the facts must be faced so change and healing can begin.

AFFIRMATION

I am willing to endure pain today knowing that greater consciousness is on the other side of the pain.

JOURNAL EXERCISE

■   *Write down your responses to the following questions:*

1. *How do you try to distract yourself from your pain?*

2. *How do you deal with your pain directly?*

3. *How do others in your life find distraction from pain?*

4. *How do others deal directly with their pain?*

5. *What can you learn from your experiences and those of the people around you?*

6. *What are you willing to do today to become more conscious and to work on your inner self?*

58

MOVING THROUGH YOUR ANGER

Holding onto anger is like grasping a hot coal with the intent of throwing it at someone else; you are the one who gets burned.

~ The Buddha

Anger, one of the five stages of the entire grief process (along with denial, bargaining, depression, and acceptance), is normal and healthy. Anger is not only healthy, it is even considered to be an essential part of grieving. As uncomfortable as it can be to feel heightened levels of anger for an extended period, it is crucial to allow yourself to go through this phase.

Anger can be a very scary experience, regardless of whether it's your own anger or anger that is directed at you. For this reason, many people try hard to avoid it. Yet feeling angry is not wrong. It's what you do with your anger that determines whether it is constructive or destructive.

Using anger to stand up for yourself and to take care of yourself and your children can actually serve you well. That is constructive. Screaming and raging can damage relationships and self-esteem and is, therefore, destructive.

Another expression of anger not discussed as often as screaming and raging is the kind of anger in which someone seethes for years. This is the person who cannot get over the wrongs that have been done to her or him, and self-identifies as a victim. Although it may feel powerful to wield your anger over someone, it is actually quite disempowering, because you are spending your valuable time and energy thinking about the person with whom you are angry. The act of focusing on that other person is sometimes called "giving your power away."

Because divorce is such an intense experience, fraught with feelings of rejection, failure, and mistrust, it is a situation in which people have the potential to stay angry for years. They may resent the fact that they have had to return to work, or that they now have the burden of child care responsibilities, or that they have no hope of having children anymore and feel that they "wasted" valuable years with their ex-spouse. Perhaps they trusted someone who was untrustworthy and now their anger is directed at themselves as well as at their spouse.

There are endless scenarios and reasons why people can become—and stay—angry, but if you do stay angry, you should know that the toxic emotion is in you and the other person may have no clue that you are feeling the way you do. It is always in your best interest to move beyond feeling high levels of anger.

AFFIRMATION

I am moving through my anger today.

JOURNAL EXERCISE

The following questions are the same questions you answered in chapter 9, "Anger." Without referring back to the answers you wrote down earlier, answer the same questions now:

- *Write about people other than yourself whom you feel anger toward: whom are you mad at and why?*

- *Next, write a list of the ways in which you feel disappointed with or angry at yourself.*

- *Are any of the items on these two lists the same?*

- *What do you feel you have learned as a result of errors you have made?*

- *What do you need in order to heal from this experience?*

- *How do the answers you wrote today compare with the answers you wrote for chapter 9?*

EXERCISE

You may want to revisit the questions in the journal exercise above every three months (no less) to see what movement, if any, there has been in coming to resolution with your anger or hurt feelings.

If you find that you are not moving through these intense emotions, I strongly advise that you seek out an anger management course or some professional guidance in order to process what you are experiencing on a deeper level. There may be some "stuck places" that you cannot heal on your own. It's okay to ask for help.

59

SETTING GOALS

Be not afraid of growing slowly, be afraid only of stand-ing still.

~ Chinese proverb

For some people, divorce feels like a failure, not so much because the marriage didn't work, but because being divorced means being single again, having to downsize, perhaps take in a roommate, fend for themselves, and live much as they did before marriage.

It certainly can be humbling to have to go backwards; however, as with many changes in life, sometimes you do have to go backwards in order to move forward. The important thing to keep in mind is that the decline in the standard of living you may experience as a result of your divorce doesn't have to be permanent. Divorce can open the way toward a better living situation, a more satisfying job or career path, and even a healthier relationship.

But the process of getting from where you are to where you want to be can be long and slow, and this is source of great frustration. Given a choice, most people would rather breeze through the dissolution and get on with their new lives. The slow personal growth (which at times can feel like no growth) can be agonizing. But no one is given the choice. Getting a divorce is like living through an earthquake with a magnitude of 7 on the Richter scale; it makes sense that it takes a long while to rebuild.

Setting goals for yourself is a helpful tool for reconstructing your life and helps you stay aware that change is happening. Working toward and meeting realistic goals, such as "In two years, I aim to finish my schooling for my new career," or "I'll live in my current situation until my youngest is in junior high school, and then I'll move to a new town," provides a sense of accomplishment. Although nothing in the immediate here and now will have changed, you will likely feel empowered because you have a plan, and you know things will change and be more to your liking in time.

You are growing; perhaps not at the rate you might grow if you had more time, money, and energy. However, as time passes and you get more information about what's in store for you in your future, you can continue to revise and refine your goals.

Setting goals is a powerful tool in setting your intention to move toward the place you want to be.

AFFIRMATION

I am moving toward my goals today.

JOURNAL EXERCISE

- Write out a list of postdivorce goals you have for yourself. Next to each goal, put a time line, such as one year, eighteen months, and so forth.

- Whenever you feel frustrated that you are not where you want to be, check this list and ask yourself the following questions:

  1. Am I any closer to my goals?

  2. Is there something I can do today or tomorrow to move closer to my goals?

  3. Do I need to modify my goals in some way?

  4. Are there outside resources I can call on for assistance in reaching my goals? If so, what are those resources and how can I access them?

  5. What do I need to work on accepting today?

EXERCISE

The following Serenity Prayer by Reinhold Niebuhr is a wonderfully helpful prayer that you may want to say during these frustrating times.

> God (or Higher Power or Universe), grant me the serenity to accept the things I cannot change, the courage to change the things I can, and the wisdom to know the difference.

Recite this prayer as often as you need to.

60

LIFE AS IT IS, NOT AS YOU WOULD HAVE IT BE

We must be willing to let go of the life we have planned,
so as to have the life that is waiting for us.

~ E. M. Forster

When most people get married, they believe it will be forever. After all, that's what it's supposed to be. Yet you (and perhaps your spouse too) must now accept the fact that your marriage is over. Depending on your circumstances, facing this new reality can be quite challenging.

It's a normal part of grieving to wonder about the future you won't have together and mourn the loss of what might have been. You should expect to have regretful thoughts and allow them to be part of your divorce experience to a certain extent.

Many people who don't fully recover from divorce or whose recovery takes a very long time are those who don't accept that their vision for the future won't happen. On some basic level, they may believe that if they don't give their attention to the divorce, then their spouse will change his or her mind and everything between them will magically work out.

Continuing to engage in wishful thinking around the relationship you had with your spouse will prevent you from being present in the moment and from moving on with your life.

Accepting a reality you don't want to face is an enormous challenge, regardless of whether the reality has to do with your marriage, your career, your health, or some other important area of your life. This is what's called "living life on life's terms," and it requires a certain amount of emotional maturity.

As with any of the cards life has dealt you, you don't have to like them, but you do have to accept them, unless, of course, you can change them. In most cases you cannot.

One trap I've seen some people fall into is thinking that if they could just understand what happened or why things happened the way they did, then they could accept the reality. Although it sometimes can help to make sense of what occurred, understanding why something happened doesn't change the fact that it did happen. Acceptance, therefore, can't be based on waiting for a satisfactory explanation or on your understanding of the events that have taken place.

To accept something, you must adopt the attitude that is best stated by this short sentence: What has happened has happened. If and when you find yourself imagining how things "should have been" with your spouse, do your best to accept your current circumstances. There is nothing wrong with imagining a brighter future when it's done as a goal-setting exercise and not as an escape into fantasy.

AFFIRMATION

I accept life on life's terms today.

JOURNAL EXERCISE

- *Write a list of the events or aspects of your divorce that you are having trouble accepting.*

- *How is this event or aspect of your divorce different from what you expected or hoped would happen?*

- *What is your understanding of why various events or aspects of your divorce happened?*

- *Does this understanding change how you feel about it or how much your accept?*

- *What do you feel needs to happen in order for you to accept those events or aspects of your divorce?*

- *Is there anything you can do to receive healing about the events or aspects of your divorce?*

One healthy and releasing exercise would be to write a letter to your spouse (or anyone else toward whom you hold bad feelings) expressing your anger, disappointment, or feelings of betrayal. You may want to save the letter and refer to it at a later date as a measure of whether your acceptance of the situation has increased.

61

BLESSING YOUR SPOUSE

Forgiveness allows you to be at peace with the person you chose to be with by repairing any damage from when you were mistreated. It is how grief resolves itself and turns from the past to the future.

~ Fred Luskin

To arrive at the place where you wish no ill will toward your spouse is to be empowered and free from the painful times you've endured. Wishing your spouse well is a step beyond this. However, depending on where you are in your process and what you have been through, the thought of blessing your spouse may feel completely impossible.

Although you certainly don't ever have to forgive your spouse for past hurts, there is something to be said for blessing someone you have been through a major part of your life with, and perhaps with whom you share children. Blessing does not mean condoning any pain your spouse may have caused you and it doesn't even mean you have to like this person. It simply means that you sincerely hope that your spouse finds peace and happiness (just as you wish that for yourself).

Reaching this level of detachment is not an easy feat, and it is not something that can be imposed on you. If you don't feel it, don't be hard on yourself and don't try to force the issue. If you never arrive at this place emotionally, that doesn't mean you haven't completed your divorce recovery. This step is the equivalent to whipped cream on a sundae. You don't really need it, but it adds a delicious layer to the entire process.

Staying open-minded to the thought of forgiving your spouse is what this section is suggesting, not as a benefit to your spouse, but because getting to this place emotionally and mentally enhances *your* life. You will feel better when you no longer harbor grudges, resentments, and pain. You will feel better when you hold good thoughts for another person. It makes life easier for you, in some cases for your spouse, and certainly for those around you.

AFFIRMATION

I wish my spouse peace and happiness.

JOURNAL EXERCISE

- *Write down a list of wrongs your spouse has committed against you. Keep this list in a place where you can refer to it from time to time (perhaps every six months or so). As time goes by, check the list to see if there are any wrongs for which you can now forgive your spouse. If and when you can forgive, cross that one off your list and write about how or why you were able to forgive this wrong.*

- *Write about the differences you notice in yourself (your mind, body, and spirit) between when you were feeling angry versus how forgiveness feels.*

Note: *If over time, you are not crossing anything off your list, it may mean that you are unconsciously holding onto your pain. You may want to speak with a friend or a divorce professional to get some guidance as to whether you are stuck somewhere in the divorce process.*

You have come to the end of this book, but not necessarily to the end of your divorce recovery. I hope you've found this book to be a valuable tool.

Read the entire book, or particular sections, as many times as you need to and do the writing and meditations as often as you need to.

I wish you ultimate peace and strength as you grow through your divorce transition into the next chapter of your life.

Susan Pease Gadoua

Susan Pease Gadoua, LCSW, is founder and executive director of the Transition Institute of Marin in the greater San Francisco Bay Area, an agency that provides coaching, therapy, and workshops to people who are at some stage of marital dissolution. She also works with couples and adolescents. Gadoua's first book, *Contemplating Divorce*, appeared on the *San Francisco Chronicle* bestseller list.